His Light at the End of Every Tunnel Revealed

Raymond L. Thompson

NP

Thompson/New Harbor Press
1601 Mt. Rushmore Rd, Ste 3288
Rapid City, SD 57701
www.newharborpress.com

His Light at the End of Every Tunnell Revealed/Thompson —1st ed.
ISBN 978-1-63357-431-1

Contents

Introduction

THIS IS THE STORY of the breadth and depth of God's mercy and forgiveness toward all Christians, believers and nonbelievers, whether Jewish or Gentile, and myself, as revealed to me in my life for the past seventy-five years.

I recently heard a brother in Christ say the Bible is God's autobiography written by men with faults, from the creation of all things in Genesis to the end described in Revelation.

GOD has no beginning or end but for our finite understanding of things, I think His story relates to us by Him stating that He is the Alpha and Omega, first and last, and is forever, hence, "I am that I am." Jesus is the exact image of God. This story is Jesus' autobiography assigned to me.

This is not easy to write. It is not a list of excuses or justifications for my mistakes nor is it a boast of how much God did through me during my life. Also, it is not a boast of how tough I once was or am today.

It is a very detailed testimony to how wonderful Jesus, my Messiah, has been to me from my early years to my salvation during my backslidden years, detailing His disciplines and mercies in my life, and through His merciful restoration. It is not an assumption that I have suddenly arrived at the knowledge of God and Yeshua, Jesus, His son, because I have not. Also, as only He can do, He has shown me how all my life events are linked together in progression.

It's a detailed story of significant events or anecdotes in my life and how God worked all things together for good through my mistakes, failures, and "successes." I pray because of the depth of my sin, it will liberate Christians and others, Jews and non-Jews, who are struggling to know God and to live a positive, fruitful, and wonderful life hearing His voice as the Scriptures teach we can. It is a story of how His kindness overcame my rebellion, sometimes intentional, and brought me back to the sheepfold in His loving arms. It is my story, different, but not unlike many others, describing how He carried me from the broad road leading to destruction back to the narrow road leading to life.

It is full of details, mercies in disciplines, and restorations I have never revealed to old friends, new friends, and even family. It may not be an easy read, but I pray with all my heart that, as you do, you will see how wonderfully awesome and merciful God is, to the Jew first and also to the Gentile and to me. I am not the exception.

It is the story of God's heart toward me as I labored to know who He is and understand why I repeatedly failed, suffered for my failures, and failed again until I came to understand what He was trying to say to me.

It is the story of what God has done to steer me to decide to change my mind or repent and come into His glorious light.

I offer no apologies for what I am sharing, only apologies to everyone I have harmed during my life. I ask forgiveness.

I was born a Gentile, am still a Gentile; but, today, believe I am grafted into the commonwealth of Israel as an unnatural branch and, as a result, am able to share in the blessings God has for His natural branches, the Jewish people to whom I am grateful.

I dedicate this to my former wife Deborah, and my children, who were initially blessed and then suffered as I ran from God, the Christian friends I may have harmed, as well as anyone else I have known who I have not seen to be able to ask for forgiveness.

Some names may have been changed or abbreviated to protect anonymity or left out intentionally. I may have forgotten some, but the details are remembered. I have taken great caution to ensure that I convey the positive influence people have had on my life story regardless of their own personal struggles. Who am I to judge anyone? The sun rises and sets on all of us on earth regardless of our struggles. It is my story, not others'; so, I only convey the deep details of my life and the impacts others have had on me.

My goals in writing this are as follows:

- To reveal God's mercy and grace in every significant event in my life, not others';
- To be gut wrenchingly honest about my failings and God's successes and mercies in my life;
- To not condemn anyone, whether a drug dealer or user, pastor or former wife;
- To speak to anyone in any walk of life, black or white, Jew or Gentile, or of any nationality who has struggled with drugs and sexual sins;
- To be a book of hope for those who read it, since I am no exception;
- To provide some humor for the reader for such a dark and hidden subject as sexual sins beginning with lust of the eyes in a world that flaunts sex but refuses to be honest and admit that many of us are obsessed or possessed by it;
- To show the progression of the sins of lust of the eyes and flesh and drugs if not addressed at the cross of Christ and to reveal my story of God's progression of restoration, where I am not the exception; and,

- To share the glorious message of salvation.

To conclude this introduction, I will explain where my heart lies today. In 2008, I was diagnosed with prostate cancer and treated with radiation. It returned, but I have refused debilitating hormone therapy. This is the only remaining medical treatment option I have. Due to the side effects and moral principles, I refused this treatment. The cancer has not spread, but I have also recently been diagnosed and treated for bladder cancer and melanoma on my back. I believe Isaiah 53, which says "by His stripes, we are healed" and I believe I am healed. Whether the doctors say it or not.

I have not felt better in years: first, in my heart and soul, and, second, in my body. At seventy-five, I still walk, ride a bike, paddle around in my pool, clean my house, mow, shovel snow, and cook. However, my first and primary activity is worship, prayer, reading the Scripture, and sharing the love God has given me with others by exemplary living. I am learning to be kind and love others with the love God has given me. This is not because I am working so much harder. I do not merit God's favor but I have received it. This is grace. I am not the exception. I have been forgiven much, so I love much.

Psalm 90:10 says we are granted seventy years in this life and eighty if we are strong. My sole goal for however many years I have left, being seventy-five now, is to walk hand in hand with my Lord and Savior, my Messiah, Yeshua, Jesus. I want to know Him and not merely talk about Him. I want to experience His daily presence in my life and actually see and be aware of His glorious work. I am now dedicated to serving Him. My prayer is that this book would be published and made available to everyone interested in reading my story, which is really His story through me, after my departure.

I assure you, this story is not fiction. I pray and worship the Lord every night and morning before writing. Then, often, during the middle of the night, God brings to my remembrance anecdotes, including names and the many details of each, which I write down and are included for believability as well as to remind me of all the Lord has done in my life. He also opened my mind to understand what He did that protected me and taught me, including the Bible verses appropriate for each lesson He taught me. Then, I cry old man baby tears of joy and either go back to sleep or wake up.

Finally, in the acknowledgments are short excerpts dedicated to individuals who have greatly blessed me with their friendship, concern, prayers, and love, whether still around or passed away. They deserve much credit for the change of events in my life and I pass the blessings God has granted me on to them as well.

Like me, every person on earth has a story like this, and God is able and willing to open everyone's eyes to see His wonderful works in all of us if we acknowledge His Word as being true in its entirety and pray and ask Him to speak to us through it.

Use an Internet search to reference people's names as well as Bible verses when I do not include them. Asking, seeking, and finding God by searching is a blessing He wants all of us to experience.

Here we go. It is OK to both laugh and cry. The anecdotes are mostly sequential, with some being humorous, at least to me. They should be read sequentially to understand the progression of Gods' work in my story and the miracles He has done. Of course, this is your choice.

CHAPTER 1

My First Birth and the Years That Follow

My Origins, Was I a Mistake?

YES, I WAS PRIVILEGED; I was born. I am quite a few years younger than both my brother and sister, so I always wondered if I was a mistake. One family member told me that my uncle was living with my parents after returning from the Korean War, and they wanted him to be on his own, so they had another child, me.

My mom and dad were like many parents from the Des Moines, Iowa, area where I lived. They were hardworking, depression survivors, who both graduated from Drake University. Well, Dad was a few hours short, so, he refused to enroll and pay tuition for one more semester for a few credits to get his degree. He later became Vice President for Valley Bank and Trust Company for years. Mom was a stay-at-home mom, working hard to raise all three of us.

I only had two grandparents I knew as a youth. My great-grandfather on my mother's side was William Meyer. I only knew him when I was very young, but do know that he was

President, for a while, of the New Reformed Jewish Temple, then located at 51st and Grand in Des Moines. As a little tyke, I sat on his lap while he smoked an old stogie, a cigar. My grandmother, and the only other grandparent I knew, was Myrtle Meyer Eldred. She authored a nationally syndicated column, daily from 1920 until 1965, published in over one hundred papers throughout the United States and Canada, called *Your Baby and Mine*. She wrote two books, one with the same title, and the second, *Worried Women*. She lived in the Bolton apartments across from my grade school, Greenwood in Des Moines, Iowa. In her early years, she was a screen editor for MGM in New York. She was listed in Who's Who in America, which at the time, was a public means of recognizing people's accomplishments in life. She lived into her nineties.

Grandma was credited as being the originator of what was called "Scientific Motherhood," providing guidance and advice to mothers rearing children from birth through their teenage years. She answered thousands of letters over her life from women with questions about how to raise their children and published the most significant questions and responses much like the column "Dear Abby." She was followed by Dr. Spock. I cannot imagine how hard she worked. Her primary education was at New York University and, later, she took classes at Columbia University. She could type sixty words per minute with two fingers, faster than anyone.

Every Christmas holiday, myself, Mom, Dad, and my cousins went to Grandma's for dinner, played board games, opened presents and, of course, ate so much food we fell asleep while our parents schmoozed. My mother ghostwrote Grandma's articles later in her life for about five years.

Merry Christmas, Readers, Meet My Four-Year Old Grandson, Ray Jr.

I remembered and shuddered when she wrote her Christmas articles every year describing in detail all of her children's growth experiences, from childhood through our teen years. In around 2000, I found many of these articles online. I recently read one in particular, written in 1950.

She wrote about me: "Raymond Jr., is just past four, and now goes to nursery school. On the day he approached the school for the first time and saw the groups of noisy children, he turned to his mother. **I think I am really too young to go to school,** he said gravely. He is a thoughtful, highly imaginative and interesting child, who in not one of his four years has ever been a menace to any adult possessions. *Just wait Grandma,* He comports himself cautiously always and now is terrifically concerned with death. He states emphatically: **I never want to be dead, ever, ever.** Strange, that I don't remember the **don't want to be dead** comment, but thank you, Grandma, for all those kind words."

Here is a cover picture from my grandma's book. It is a picture of her, my brother, sister, and cousins. I am the little inquisitive one to her right looking at her big book.

The author with her grandchildren

A Serious Rebel as a Teen

My grade school years were so similar to those of Bill Bryson as written in his book, *The Thunderbolt Kid*, that I purchased three copies for my kids and told them this was my youth years as well. I attended Greenwood Grade School, which employed towering teachers. I had experienced the long descent, during fire drills, down the fire escape. I played baseball in the huge fields behind school and was in a class with one of the Butters' brothers. I went to Younker's tea room for the toys with Grandma who also wrote for the Register and Tribune like Bill's father. I had a paper route, and more like Bryson.

I was, perhaps, more like the character Katz in Bryson's books and, later, in his movie, *A Walk in the Woods*. Katz orchestrated a beer heist as a youth, but a little different than mine. One summer, I was hired by a Hamm's beer distributor in Des Moines as a warehouse assistant. Pretty important, huh? I took broken beer bottles from cases off pallets, which had arrived via piggyback truck on railroad cars, pulled the nonbroken ones out, put them back into fresh cases, and gave them to my boss, who put them back in inventory. Since I was a lifeguard other summers, during lunch breaks, I would climb up, lay flat on the rail car's topside, and get a tan.

My friends and I used to have fake IDs which we used to buy beer. These were followed by trips to a remote cornfield where we drank. One day, I decided why not stash a few unbroken extra beer bottles, not yet in inventory, from the broken cases for our trips to the field. The challenge was to get them to my friends. Well, at noon, businesses came to the warehouse to pick up their preordered beer. They drove through the warehouse, and, if my boss was away, I was the one who loaded them into their trucks or cars. You can figure the rest. My friends became really good friends at that point.

I never went to Reform School, like Katz, but should have. However, I had become a thief and rebel. Today, I realize, I was being shown the mercy from God, even at that young age.

The Straw That Could Have Broken This Camel's Back

God had foreknowledge of my life. He knew the end outcome from the beginning, but I think this story, like Paul's in the Bible, might have resulted in God looking down and saying, "I want this man for my service. Let's go to work to bring Him into the sheepfold." We don't always come into His kingdom without some crying and even kicking. There is pain in natural child birth as well as Spiritual birth.

One of my best friends in high school had a brother who won second place in the World Science Fair in Tokyo. He had built a robot in the mid-1960s that recorded and remembered its movements as it rolled through his house. There was a local radio station that broadcast a Christian program. The message delivered was always riddled with the words "hell," "damned," and "God."

The three of us concocted a plan that opened a door for satanic attacks in my life. However, God allowed it for His purposes. We recorded the show at home. Then, we spliced the words so that the preacher was cussing, not glorifying God. Then, we drove to the station's transmitter, spliced the wires, and rebroadcast the modified message while we recorded it back at home. We communicated with our ham radios in our cars while keeping watch for anyone. Funny, huh?

To this day, some fifty-five years later, I thank God, we were not caught, sent to reform school and/or federal prison. I am sure, if discovered, I would not be a licensed radio operator today. Thank you, God, for your mercy during my youth!

Ironically, I didn't know that, later in my life, I would cohost a call-in Hebrew Christian radio program with Dr. Andy Meyers, a medical doctor in Kansas City, Missouri, and Dr. Neil Weiner, an economic adviser to President Richard Nixon. Both had become Hebrew Christians.

I Was a "Headbanger"

I never found any mention of me being a "headbanger" in Grandma's articles, but as a child, when I didn't get my way, I would bang my head against the wall until I did. The following headbanging experiences during my teenage years had lifelong consequences.

On two occasions, I was in accidents where my head broke through the passenger seat front windshields of cars. This was prior to seatbelts.

The first, at seventeen, I had taken my dad's new used car to pick up my girlfriend who had been issued a learner's permit to drive. I drove down John Lynde Road, a dark crooked street surrounded by big oak trees in Des Moines with very little traffic. I stopped the car and said, "Do you want to drive?" She tried.

It took about fifteen seconds after she got behind the wheel, and stepped on the gas too hard, for us to careen into a really big oak tree, totaling my dad's new used car. I survived with a huge gash in my face, and glass in my head. However, on the positive side, for the first time, I got to ride in an ambulance to the hospital where I was stitched up.

Then, several years later, during a Christmas holiday break from college, my now older, but just as immature friends at the time, decided to do car doughnuts on the fresh snow in a nearly empty Piggly Wiggly grocery store parking lot. Of course, I was in the passenger seat behind the front window and, again, the window welcomed me through it with a similar result.

Even though I was hardheaded, I was very fortunate to survive those accidents. God had shown His mercy to me. But, there were consequences that probably have remained to this day. These include tinnitus, a constant ringing like locust buzzing sound in my ears, as well as obsessive-compulsive disorder, extreme depression, and psychomotor epilepsy. I did not discover these problems until later.

Short Definitions for Easy Writing and Reading

Writing this is difficult for me, but blatantly honest.

What are the unmentionables? I am using this word to cover a bunch. It's much easier for myself and the reader.

The unmentionables include:

- Lust of the eyes and flesh
- Pornography
- Masturbation
- Adultery, which includes fornication
- Prostitutes, including escorts
- Idolatry

For me, they are all accompanied by perverse behavior, sexual deviancy, drugs and alcohol use, lying, stealing, anger at myself and others, criticism, resentment, bitterness, and cursing.

If I forgot any, read on and add to the list.

D stands for drugs and includes:

- Alcohol
- Marijuana
- Hash
- Crack
- Cocaine powder
- Speed
- Opium
- Heroin

<u>NA stands for Narcotics Anonymous</u>, a recovery program like Alcoholics Anonymous, Both are twelve-step programs. AA was started by Bill Wilson and Marty Mann.

<u>Slide refers to a progressive and painful falling away</u> from the living God into discipline for my behavior. It is also called "back-sliding." If used in the NA context, it refers to a return to D.

Preface to the Good, Bad, Ugly, and the Unmentionables

I need to digress to talk about what God has shown me about the dark experiences in my life. When writing, I often use Bible Scriptures God has shown me to explain His work in me. I spent about the last eighteen years reading a chapter a day during breakfast on an HP Jornada Pocket PC located on my kitchen counter.

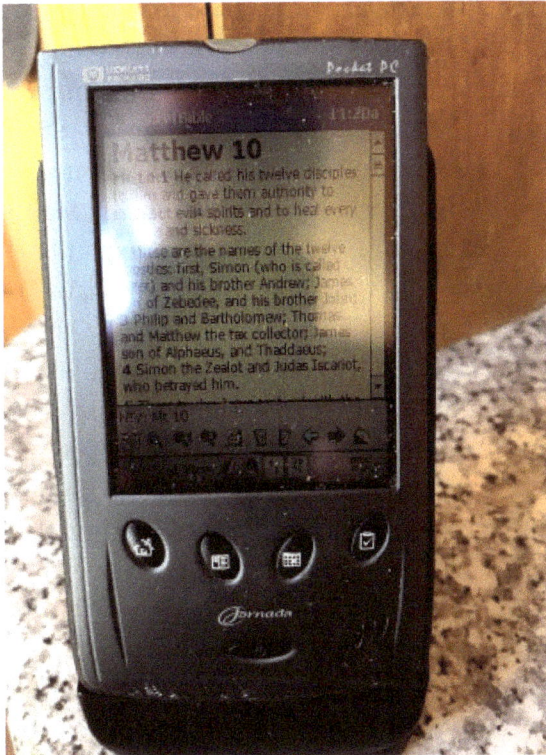

It was my daily spiritual food. I read the Old Testament, from Genesis through Malachi, three times and the New Testament, from Matthew through Revelation, ten to twelve times. I also prayed and researched specific topics during the day. For example, I read on topics like money, marriage, or death.

I knew some Scripture Bible reference numbers like John 3:16, etc., but never was able to do hard-core memorization. For me and me only, God showed me that if I had, I would boast, with pride of my great knowledge which, of course, I did anyway. That boastful knowledge had no real impact in changing anyone's life. So, if you recognize a Bible verse in my story, slap it into an Internet search, as I do, and you should find it. Besides, to know God, the Bible says, "Seek, and you shall find, knock, and it shall be opened to you." God required me to work, to know Him, not be handed understanding on a silver platter. I am a seeker and a knocker. The Bible also says that the Holy Spirit shall teach us all things, and bring all things to our remembrance that He said to us. I am nothing special. He does this for everyone who seeks, knocks, and reads Scripture and He does it for me.

In the Ten Commandments, God says, "Thou shall not commit Adultery," which includes fornication. In Matthew, in the Beatitudes, God, His son, Yeshua, Jesus, expands on this and says, if you look upon a woman lustfully, you have already committed adultery with her in your heart. Also, He says if your eye causes you to stumble, pluck it out and if your right hand causes you to stumble, cut it off. Twice, he explains further that it is more profitable for one of our members to perish, than our whole body be cast into hell. DON'T DO THIS literally. They are written to emphasize the gravity of these sins and their effect on our relationship with Him. The Bible also says, "All have sinned and fallen short of the Glory of God."

If we are honest, regardless of our religious beliefs or religious titles, myself and most men as well as women, are guilty of these sins in God's court of law. We are tempted, or bombarded, in these areas throughout our lives through television ads, Super Bowl halftime shows, Internet ads, music videos, magazines, people at the gym, pictures of people, and more. Ignoring the Ten Commandments, which is supernaturally written on our stony hearts, sears our consciences like a hot iron.

We ignore the commands because we experience guilt and, over time, if not addressed, this opens the door to all kinds of problems, and real discipline in our lives. It did for me. The seared conscience eases the feelings of guilt and ultimately produces an acceptance of the sin. In our minds, we justify these thoughts and accept them as the new normal and the way it is. We rationalize by thinking I am the same as everyone else, why worry about it. This makes me feel good. This is the result of being seared. If we are completely honest, it is a huge dilemma for many of us.

I could not stop due to my upbringing, the way I dealt with pain, and my wrong beliefs about sex, until I became aware of how much Christ loves me. I had to see that love throughout my life, believe that His heart is a heart of mercy not judgment, and realize that He has something much more fulfilling and exciting for me than sex and drugs.

I have attended a number of larger well-known churches in my life and had been friends with many pastors and lay people who are well-known but who have fallen, like myself, into these sins. I have no excuses today. I have no justifications or alibis left. I am guilty as charged. However, I have an advocate who stands before the father and pleads my case. He committed no sin although He had been tempted in every area as we are. Therefore, He is righteous and worthy to be our intermediary.

The Bible says, confess your sins (plural) to each other and pray for each other, so that you might be healed. I don't believe it is a glossed over confession. For example, I would say: "OK, Bob, I have this little sin problem of lust, please pray for me, BUT I had this great new understanding of God and here is what He showed me." Whether saved or not, most of us, like myself, in pride, minimize or hide our failures and only boast our successes to others. This is due to our fear of criticism and rejection which we deal out as judgment to others we know. We point our index fingers at the guilty, when we have three other fingers pointing back at us. The Bible says judge and you shall be judged. Guilty again! I was severely disciplined by God for years. I walked in the wilderness sinning, repenting, and sinning again, caught in what seemed like an endless downward spiral.

Like most, I was born with five fingers on both hands, with one index finger on each. Over the years, I have had two hand accidents: first, where I slammed a glass ashtray down on a table because I was angry at my second wife; and, second, when I jabbed my finger against a stationary object. Both were surgically repaired, but the ends of each index finger are bent, making it impossible for me to point directly at anyone effectively. There is the message to me.

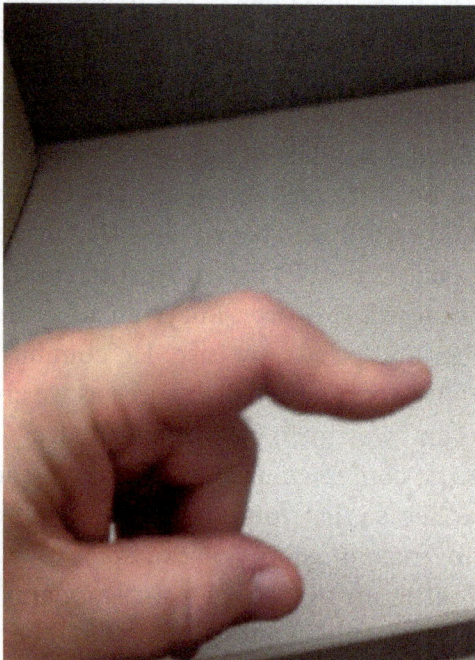

We look at the Bible and revere godly men who are our examples, like Moses, Abraham, David, Jonah, Saul (later Paul), and Cephas (later Peter). However, they ALL were once sinners. Moses, David, and Saul had each committed murder. Abraham married his servant, thinking it would fulfill God's promise. Moses, in anger, killed an Egyptian and struck the rock (a type of our Messiah) when Israel did not listen, and David lusted, then killed Bathsheba's husband in order to marry her. Saul murdered Christians including Stephen. Jonah, like me, ran from God. Cephas, Peter, with a sword, cut off a Roman centurion's ear when he was arresting Yeshua, Jesus. He did this after he believed Jesus was his Messiah.

Each was disciplined to a measure for their actions. Moses did not enter the Promised Land with the Israelites. Abraham's first son was Ishmael, the father of all the Arab nations which are still a thorn in the nation's side today. David suffered major ridicule and criticism from his people. Jonah was swallowed by a whale. Saul lost his sight for a period before his conversion. Cephas was rebuked by Jesus as Jesus healed the ear of one who led Him to His death and later denied that he knew Jesus three times after He was crucified.

God showed each mercy. They ALL became deeply honest as an example for us to follow and changed their minds (repented) of their actions. The results and their restoration were revealed and are recorded in the Bible by our loving, merciful, forgiving God. Moses became the pillar of the Jewish faith, gave us the Law, and performed many miracles. Abraham had a son, Isaac, though His given wife, Sarah, and became the father of many nations. Jonah became a prophet of God and preached to the inhabitants of Nineveh who later repented of their sins. Peter became the "rock," one of the twelve disciples and a pillar of the Christian faith. Paul wrote much of the New Testament which we have today. David gave us the Psalms which enable us to pray deeply from our hearts and sing wonderful songs to God.

Their stories are all written in God's autobiography as an example for us to follow. Ask God, seek God, and you will find Him in your portion of God's autobiography. I did, and, believe me, I am no exception. Like I said, I make no excuses today. Were they believers in God when their sins were forgiven? I am sure they were.

Time for Some Good News

The Bible says God's mercies endure forever through Yeshua, Jesus, our Savior, to the Jew first and also to the Greek or Gentile. The Bible also says, His mercies are NEW every morning.

Like the paschal lamb sacrificed at the annual Jewish Passover with its blood being placed on the doorposts to protect Israel from God's judgment, God sacrificed His son Yeshua, Jesus, by sending Him into the world in human form to live a sinless life, and be sacrificed by the shedding of His blood on the Cross so that we can have it placed on the doorposts of our hearts. This sacrifice was intended for the Jew first and also the Greek or Gentile. The difference between these two sacrifices, the lamb and Jesus, is that God brought His son, Jesus, who was tempted in everything as we are, but without sin, back to life. We no longer needed an annual lamb sacrifice. His sacrifice was accomplished once for all of us and is eternal.

The Bible says, He descended into Hades, took the keys to death and Hades from the tempter, Satan, and ascended into Heaven to stand in the gap as our sacrificial lamb forever atoning for our sins. I had to believe this or I had no hope. The Bible also says He stands before His father, the judge, as an advocate mediating our case. And, for those who believe what He says in the Bible (called "having faith"), He imputes forgiveness for all our sins and wrong behavior, past, present, and future during our entire lifetime. This is called "grace" or "unmerited favor." I did not receive grace based upon what I did, but based upon my faith in Him and His words to me.

Therefore, even when I blew it over and over again, Yeshua, Jesus, forgave me. The gravity or seriousness of my sins was not the issue. I read about the thief on the cross and the examples of the patriarchs above, but it never clicked for me. God is an amazingly loving and forgiving God who is Holy, but could not tolerate sin and idolatry or anything which displaced Him from being first in my life. Yes, He is a jealous God. Why not? He created me, the world I live in, the heavens above me, and every form of life. Forget about alien distractions.

In addition, He offers me and all of us everything He has in the Bible, including:

- Faith versus constant fear
- Love for others
- Unspeakable peace
- Joy in our hearts
- Patience
- Kindness, not anger
- Mercy, not criticism toward others
- Meekness, not pride
- Gentleness, not rage and anger
- Self-control
- Healing in our bodies
- Deliverance from temptations attacking our minds
- Registry in His book of eternal life
- Residence with Him in Heaven forever
- Communications with Him

The Bible says, "My sheep hear my voice."

These are His great gifts to me, if I changed my mind or repented and chose to become His friend. Of paramount importance,

I had to choose to believe His message to me, in His Word, the Bible.

Without Faith or believing His Word, the Bible says it is impossible to please God. It also says, faith comes by hearing and hearing by the Word of the Messiah, Christ, so I needed to both read and think about it or meditate on it. I needed to sit back, relax, reject my desire to watch TV constantly, use my iPhone or laptop every moment, go shopping, worry, fret, and do anything else which distracted me from Him. I also needed to pray, ask Him to speak to me, realizing He is hearing everything I say or do. He did this for me, and He will do it for you.

I no longer live alone; He lives with me and resides in me through His Holy Spirit. I daily experience His presence and fellowship. He teaches me about everything good, bad, ugly, and unmentionable in my life, and how He has worked those things together for good in me. The darkness in me has become light. The light bulb drove it away. He no longer judges me in those areas in my life. Who am I to criticize anybody?

Experiencing Him and His kindness freed me from the unmentionables, and all D. There is nothing on this earth that compares to experiencing His fullness in my life. His presence is better than any D or unmentionable things and any relief I got from anything I obsessed over. There is no comparison. He also restored all that has been stolen from me by the canker worm or Satan. He did it for me and is still doing it for me in other areas of life. I am not the exception. He will do this for anyone.

Now, I am ready to share the rest of the progression of God's story in my life.

How I Learned to Feel Good and Numb My Frustrations and Anxiety

Actually, the title is not correct, since feeling good and numbing out frustrations the way I did only led to feeling worse and more pain and frustrations along with hurting others. I would have been better off taking Dilantin and Librium or Elavil.

Around the age of twelve, I learned that I could feel really good by committing the first stage of the unmentionables. *Playboy* was my magazine of choice. I don't remember ever being told about the birds and the bees. My Congregational church exposure involved my mom and dad driving me to church, dropping me off, and returning home. I sang in the choir, and even played the clarinet to the tune of the "When the Go Marching In" at a Christmas pageant. Church membership was achieved by sitting with the pastor for two long days listening to church doctrine. I admit, I fell asleep during those sessions. The minister never visited my parents to reach out to them. But, annually, he stopped by to collect church dues.

I was never told that sex was to be reserved for marriage or how to deal with my perverse thoughts and desires, and they were perverse. It was always taboo to discuss. The unmentionables were a tension reliever for my failures in high school English, French, and other topics. When I began to date in high school, my goal was to first have sex, then get to know the person I was dating. That never worked for me.

In high school, some of my friends and I drank a lot. We also smoked weed and a tan form of opiated hash. We either did this in the bedroom of one friend or the cornfields and, one time, later, in high school, at a bar, entering with fake IDs, on the corner of University Avenue and Polk Boulevard in Des Moines. One friend had a cat. On one occasion, at my friend's house, we were smoking in his bedroom with the cat sitting next to us on the bed; and, after puff number one, the cat curled up his back and started hissing. We all backed into a corner for about fifteen minutes until it finally stopped. That should have been a warning sign to me, but it wasn't. I had no foundation training of morality.

In the 1990s, I found many of my grandma's articles online. I read and read to find articles on the unmentionables that she might have written. Forty-five years of daily articles is hard to get through and I had only several dozen published ones, so I assumed that was a taboo topic for her, not to be discussed; thank the good Lord for me. I really didn't want Grandma to write her Christmas articles about my masturbation problems.

Life's Consequences and Denial of My Problems

In 1967, after flunking out at Kansas University, as will be discussed later, I returned home to Des Moines to live with my parents and face the draft to fight in Vietnam. I joined the Naval Reserves with training to become a radioman.

Most of my old friends had become smashing successes in life. Two had become pharmacists, four became lawyers—one a criminal lawyer and the second a business lawyer, a the third became a well-known immigration lawyer, one became a federal lawyer serving during the Obama administration—one graduated from University of Pennsylvania from the Wharton School of Business and became a professor, one graduated from West Point and became an Army officer and a crack shot with a pistol, and two more entered the world of information technology, which I later entered as well.

Needless to say, I viewed myself as a failure not only to my parents, who paid for my education at Kansas University (KU), but to myself. This became an excuse to numb myself with pot and the unmentionables until something happened. I was arrested and charged with indecent exposure near my former high school. My life was spiraling downward. The tinnitus I had as a result of my earlier accidents had become worse, and I no longer seemed to be able to handle any stress, so I sought help from a neurologist. An EEG revealed that I had "psychomotor epilepsy," a disease that manifests its ugly head through outbursts of anger, depression, and, yes, sometimes, as in my case, sexual deviancy. I was prescribed Dilantin and Librium and, later, Elavil for treatment, which turned me into a zombie.

I was released from the Navy Reserve with an honorable medical discharge before ever being called up to Vietnam. Below is a picture of this diagnosis included as a part of my service record.

Nevertheless, I thought to myself, how could I ever get a job as a zombie without a degree, with epilepsy and a record? I think Dad knew someone that got my record purged. So, I stopped taking the medications and went into denial, as though nothing ever occurred. I stuffed, or hid, the unmentionables from everyone as I had been taught to do when I was much younger. I don't remember ever telling my first wife about these things. To add to my problems, when I finally was able to get work at Blue Cross Blue Shield as a Manager Trainee, my boss sold me weed.

Secular Education, Successes and Failures and My Jewish Wedding

After a wild and crazy high school experience in 1964, with only average grades, I was accepted to KU where my cousin Tom was attending. I pledged Sigma Nu, his fraternity as well, went through hell week, and began my college journey. Our Sigma Nu chapter was proud that prior members included William Inge, a playwright and novelist, and Ron Evans, one of the early astronauts who flew moon missions. He remained on the command ship. After leaving Kansas University being a ham operator, I wrote to him asking if he had any technical training manuals on radio communications. He sent one to me and, of course, I lost it during later years.

I also had the pleasure of meeting Jim Ryun, the Olympic runner who ran the first four-minute mile. He lived in Naismith Hall where I lived one semester when our fraternity was being renovated. Later, Debbie, my first wife, and I had the blessing of sitting next to him and his wife at a Second Chapter of Acts concert and even later he became a staff member of our church, Full Faith Church of Love. His life and running skills always inspired me to keep running until I finished the race of life.

I majored in Electrical Engineering because in high school I had become a ham radio operator as mentioned above. I minored in Mathematics. I dated with the same goals that I had in high school: sex first, relationship afterwards. After three years, I flunked out having failed Calculus 3.

I returned to my hometown of Des Moines and, after three years of college with two years of transferable credits, I was accepted to Drake University where I met my first wife Deborah, Debbie, and mother of my kids. She was Jewish, and from Skokie, Illinois, which had one of the highest population of Holocaust survivors in the United States. I met her through her pledge mother, Maggie, whom I knew in high school and dated briefly at Drake. Debbie was beautiful. We got along well, and I loved her sorority, Alpha Epsilon Phi. One year they awarded me the prestigious award of Phi Guy of the Year. I was the first Goyim (Gentile) Phi Guy of the Year.

I attended Drake University in the evening and worked during the day; and, in 1972, I finally earned my degree in Business Management. During this time, I lived at home with my parents until just prior to getting engaged. On July 5, 1970, we were married at the Blackstone Hotel in Chicago. We had only found two rabbis in Chicago who would marry us. Interestingly, my half-Jewish grandmother advised against our marriage.

It was the traditional Jewish wedding with a full orchestra, chuppah covered with flowers, and the traditional breaking of the glass followed by dancing the hora. We also danced to Greek music since Debbie's mom was Greek, although she was raised Jewish. My family looked on with amazement, since they had never been to such an event. The traditional marriages they had experienced were in churches followed by a reception at a home or a local restaurant.

I received lots of envelopes that day filled with cash. I could not wait to return to our room and count it. The cash paid for our honeymoon to Bermuda and lots of furniture. In Bermuda, we stayed in a beachside room overlooking the ocean. Upon my first dive into the surf, my wedding band, which I had purchased by selling all my ham radio equipment, slipped off in the surf, never to be found. It was replaced later. Perhaps this was another sign something was wrong.

My first job after attending Kansas University and returning to Des Moines to attend Drake University was at Blue Cross Blue Shield in the late 1960s. My boss was Wes C. I remember two anecdotes at this point.

The first occurred one morning upon arrival to work. As I walked into the entrance, I was passed by a man running through the hall past me. I thought maybe he is just late for a meeting. When I arrived in the office after exiting the elevator, I saw my boss hiding behind his desk with bullet holes in the glass in front of his desk, and one of my coworkers hiding under her desk with blood dripping down. I do not remember, but I don't believe she died. I thank the Lord I had not arrived a few minutes earlier.

After working there for a while, the existing manager left, and his slot was opened for hire. Wes C. and I had applied. There was a great need for racial equality at the time, and Wes C. was probably more qualified than I, so he got the job. We became friends as well as coworkers. I had been engaged to Debbie during that period, but I also had an affair with a coworker that cost me my job.

Debbie and I lived in Des Moines until I graduated from Drake University in 1972, when I took a better job with Funeral Security Plans (FSP) in Kansas City. I was put in charge of the Death Claims Department. This was the best I could find, and was definitely not my ultimate goal. Remember Grandma's Christmas article about me at age four? Death spooked me out.

The funeral business was a conglomerate that includes FSP, funeral homes, cemeteries, and a casket-manufacturing company. How exciting it was to regularly walk from FSP to the funeral home next door past a bunch of caskets with cadavers in some. But, the exciting part was that the youngest owner smoked weed and, at Christmas parties in Topeka, our small entourage of employees would be taken in limousines to the party smoking all the way.

I remember getting a call one day from a person who identified himself as Tony (Anthony) Civella. He asked me to tell him what a certain prearranged funeral policy paid for a nonmember of his family. I was not allowed to provide that information to anyone over the phone, so he got pretty angry. I think I hung up, and then asked a coworker named Kitty H. what to do. She informed me that he was head of the Kansas City branch of Cosa Nostra and that she would call him back. Anthony or Nicholas, not sure which, was depicted in the movie *Casino*.

I am thankful to God, today, that I did not wind up in one of the caskets in the funeral home next to FSP. God had again put death in my life and on my mind at this point.

Onward, upward, and then downward.

CHAPTER 2

My Second Spiritual Birth and the Years That Followed

Hope in the Midst of More Failure

I DID NOT FIND God by attending a church, but by reading the Bible after praying that God would open my eyes to understand it.

In 1972, my marriage was failing since I had many problems. My sister, Suzy, had become a Bible-thumping Christian. She always witnessed to us, telling us that Jesus was the Jewish Messiah and how she had been forgiven for her sins. She kept saying to me: "Pray to God in Jesus' name to reveal Himself to me, then read the Bible and He will speak to you." I didn't own a Bible, so on a shopping trip to Kmart, Debbie and I, got in an argument. I wanted to buy one of the new Living Bibles stacked near the front entrance and Debbie refused. She went shopping while I waited in the car, but when she returned with the Bible in hand, I started to believe that God might have answered my prayer. Finally, I listened to my sister, and took her advice and read my new Living Bible nightly for three months to Debbie's chagrin. She was not yet a Christian.

I also prayed that God would show me why Jews and Gentiles, having a common Old Testament, did not share the same faith.

One day, on my lunch break from work, I took my noon escape drive to the Chelsea Theater in Kansas City for a quick burlesque show and the Holy Spirit began to speak almost audibly to me. This was long before GPS. He told me to drive on a certain street, turn right, then left, and then I would arrive at a bookstore. It was in the Plaza area of Kansas City. I had no idea where I was going. He said to me, when there, ask for two books to share Jesus with your Jewish wife. They only had two books, **Michael, Michael, Why Do You Hate Me**, a testimony of a rabbi who had accepted Yeshua as His Messiah, and a book of Jewish believer testimonies written by Michael Evans. I had never been back to church from my teen years and did not have this experience at a church.

I had to stop driving while on the way because I could not stop crying. I realized I was actually hearing God speak to me! This was the beginning of my salvation. I had changed my mind, did not go to the theater, and accepted Christ into my heart. Afterwards, after crying for a long time, I returned to work but, so filled with God that I could not contain myself, I told some people why I was late from lunch. I thought to myself, they would understand, but they did not.

Like Moses coming down from Mount Sinai, I beamed. I had no veil to cover my face, but I knew it, because no one I spoke to could look at me in the eye when talking. I returned home that evening with the two books for Debbie and told her what happened. I think she thought I had gone meshugganah, crazy.

I remember praying that evening and experiencing God and His strong presence to such an extent that I had to ask God to let me rest because I could not contain in my mortal body what was happening to me. I felt like I might explode.

All my sins had been forgiven that day during my lunch break, including my smoking, foul mouth, desires for weed and the unmentionables, and desire for D. I had been born again and saved from my sins and healed of my psychomotor epilepsy at that moment. Anyone, like me, would shed buckets of tears of joy as well. I am no exception. This is the way God works His miracles in us and did in me. Behold, old things had passed away, and all things had become new as the Bible says. What was done in the dark had become light. I now understood.

However, in 1973, I lost my job at Funeral Security Plans when I refused to create a false computer statement with bogus trust balances and sign a statement that it was correct. FSP was required, in some states where they operated, to maintain nearly 100% trust balances for purchasers of their funeral plans and they had not, and were being investigated by the government. The Bible says in 2 Timothy 3:12, all who desire to live godly in Messiah, Christ, Jesus shall be persecuted. Even so, I had great peace and joy in my heart.

Debbie saw the change in my life.

She gave her life to Jesus, her Messiah, about three months later after she had her own personal encounter.

We grew in the Lord while attending a wonderful Spirit-filled church in Kansas City called Full Faith Church of Love; much larger, but much like Abundant Grace Fellowship, where I attend today. Many 1960s hippies attended Full Faith.

Debbie and I also attended a home Bible study group on 77th Street conducted by a Messianic Jewish believer named David Rose. God planted His love for the Jewish people in my heart and I walked with God for about another ten years; but, as our kids grew older, and stresses at work and home raising children increased, I began to give into the temptations and the unmentionables I had previously.

God answered Debbie and my prayers in amazing ways. One such prayer was for an old friend, Bob, who was going through a divorce and whom I had not seen since he graduated from college some five or six years earlier. We had heard through the grapevine that Bob was going through a messy divorce, so we prayed for him and, about a month later, he arrived at our doorsteps and we had a chance to pray with him personally.

I moved in the gifts of the Holy Spirit sometimes. These included faith, knowledge, healing, speaking in tongues, and discerning of spirits. I remember, one early morning, we were in bed and I sensed or discerned a dark presence of a spirit in our child's room who was crying. I verbally, out loud, cast the demon out of our house in Jesus' name. Just then, our locked back-door flew open and the wicked demon left.

My New Job Working for Sharp, Charlie

In 1974, my first daughter was born. She became the joy of my life, always happy and giggling. She made me laugh. After FSP, my new job was as Licensing Manager for Ozark National Life Insurance Company. Its President was Charlie Sharp. I had a big office, best ever, next door to the Vice President. Morrell D. Times must have been tough, since after a year of no raise, which I had been promised when hired, Charlie called a meeting of staff, and informed everyone that no one would receive any wage increases. I remember a fellow employee walking down the hall, well behind Charlie, flipping a coin over his shoulder, and popping it back in his hand with the heel of his shoe. That always brought major laughter to the staff and myself.

I had a new daughter and wife to support, and I knew God does some wonderful things. Morrell D. told me not to worry and began passing me $100 bills with every paycheck. Unfortunately, the company was investigated later for money laundering. The Treasurer took the wrap. At the time, it did not occur to me, so I kept the cash gift. God always took care of our needs. I lost that job as well.

My Miracle Job and the Miracles That Followed

Before finding work, I remember God blessing us from someone in the church with $1,000 anonymously. But, I also remember looking around curbs and gutters for spare change. God always provided exactly what we needed when were nearly out of money, but only on His time schedule.

I continued to believe God had a job for me. After searching for work for about six months, and having purchased a home on 88th Street in Overland Park, Kansas, I was at church on Sunday and Pastor Ernie preached a message entitled, "If a Man Doesn't Work, Neither Shall He Eat." I liked to eat and immediately thought He was preaching to me, so I went up for prayer. He looked at me and said, "Ray, I wasn't preaching to you," but there is a member of the church who wants to hire someone in the Credit Department of Western Auto. His name was Bruce B. I applied and was hired.

I held some odd jobs in the Credit Department when Bruce informed me that he was filming something related to his lay ministry with Tim Robertson, Pat Robertson's son.

God has gifted me with some organization skills and an ability to unite people of different backgrounds throughout my life. As a Gentile, I had performed messianic Passover Seders and the Lord moved me to discuss with Arthur Katz, a messianic Jew author, then, on sabbatical in Kansas City, with Bruce and Tim Robertson, the possibility of taping a messianic Passover Seder dinner. A messianic Passover dinner demonstrates how our Messiah, Jesus, is revealed through every element of the Passover.

All agreed, and it was later recorded for *The 700 Club*. I am not sure if it was ever aired, but God had answered the prayers of

Debbie and me. It was the first time *The 700 Club* had recorded such an event to be telecast.

Bruce and I both lost our jobs at Western Auto. When Bruce learned he was being terminated, he told me immediately so I could again begin another job search. I was so grateful for that. During that time in my life, I had met Arthur Katz, as mentioned earlier. This was not the Katz in Bryson's books. I also had the pleasure of meeting Moishe Rosen, another Messianic Jew who began the organization Jews for Jesus. I also became friends with Matthew Schwartz, a Messianic Jew whom I believe was the founder of Intercessors for Israel. He led a Passover Seder presentation at the Hyatt Regency in which I had the honor to participate. I am at the podium reciting the Shema Yisrael in this picture.

During those years, and of significant importance, I met Bob Mendelsohn, now CEO for Jews for Jesus, Australia and Asia. Bob has had an immense influence in helping in my restoration over the past two years. Through Zoom Bible studies, he has been key to helping me begin to understand the love and mercy of God in Scripture.

Each of the men mentioned above, through their godly love and kindness toward me, have contributed to my life. We are not alone in our journey in life, and we are all connected in some way. More about each of them follows, but first the rest of this anecdote.

Art Katz and I would go to coffee and discuss the Bible. He was an incredibly bold man and very openly discussed his life issues. At the time, Art had written *Ben Israel*, and was considering writing a book, later titled *The Holocaust, Where Was God*, which he penned much after my slide began. He was honest and expressed his trepidation about writing this to me when we had coffee.

New Job, New Career, and the Beginning of the Slide

In late 1976 or 1977, I was hired by the City of Olathe, Kansas, as Data Processing Manager. My career was finally taking off. This was around the time, in 1976, when my precious second daughter, Rebekah, was born. What an inspiration she has been to me to continue working hard to reach my goals in life! Rebekah was more serious than my first daughter, Rachel, and power-packed with energy to spare. When young, they shared a bunk bed in a wood-paneled bedroom in our first house with big closet doors with corkboard glued onto them.

In my new job, I trained to write mainframe computer software code called Adabas, Natural and Complete, manufactured by a company in Germany named Software AG. Initially, the City of Olathe was in a consortium agreement with Johnson County, Kansas, to use computer services, but our goal was to become independent due to the cost of using the county's computer. A little side note--our building, at the time, was built on an old dump site which some said was originally the site of the hotel in Truman Capote's "horror" book, **In Cold Blood**. Oh no, another death event!

After training, I became the manager, had my own department budget, and I developed a request for proposal sent to several big companies, including IBM, to bid on building our data center. When the bids were evaluated, I chose a company out of California called Magnuson. That didn't please IBM, and they attempted to muddy the waters and discredit our review process even though their bid was significantly higher. Nevertheless, we chose the low bidder, and proceeded to award contracts to vendors who installed raised floor, wiring, emergency alarms, and sprinkling systems for fire protection and, of course, our new mainframe computer, as well as the OS/VS1 system software and Software AG development software.

I managed staff, but also ensured all the systems were converted from the county to run on our new mainframe computer. I also programmed a number of new systems including a police records system, and Court docket system with the aid of a consultant. I also did my own creative programming including using an IBM product called GDDM, Graphical Data Display Manager, and DIME files with GeoCoordinates from the Census Bureau of all street intersections in the city.

I was one of the early programmers in the nation that graphed the city streets on a mainframe and was in the process of integrating police incident locations, fire hydrant, and water and sewer locations needing repair and other data by location in the city.

God granted me secular knowledge in IT (information technology) which sent me on business trips to Silicon Valley and other locations. I acquired the knowledge that I used later to fix systems at Partners Healthcare written in Software AG code when Y2K arrived.

I submitted papers and spoke at two Software AG International Conferences, one at the Disneyland Hotel in Anaheim. I also was recognized first in *Who's Who in the Midwest*, then *Who's Who of Emerging Leaders in America*, and finally *Who's Who in America*.

At the time, this was a big deal. Only my Grandma Eldred had done that. Finally, I had some success in my life, but the stress on me was building and I was not sanctified in many areas. As the Bible says, pride comes before the fall, and mine was coming when, at this conference, I took a drive through Hollywood and committed an unmentionable again.

The Slide Begins

I was accustomed to working late much of the time and, one evening, one of my employees was also working late in our computer room. I made an inappropriate advance and lost my job. If I remember correctly, this was about 1982.

Prior to the slide, my son, David, the comedian, was born. I wanted a son, Debbie and I discussed it and prayed and God brought it to pass. He always made us laugh, by hanging spoons from his nose and ears simultaneously.

Our family took many trips to Colorado skiing. We also traveled to the Lake of the Ozarks and Silver Dollar City in Branson, Missouri. At Silver Dollar City Amusement Park, we loved the old rides like Fire in the Hole, and we ate at one of the first Outback Steak Houses with no grass surrounding it where all employees spoke with Aussie accents.

We vacation at Disneyland in California and Disney World in Florida and regularly visited Debbie's family in Chicago. I remember driving to Disney World in Florida in an old Cadillac purchased from my dad. It lost its A/C on the way down, so we cooked during most of the trip. On the way, we played games like who can count the most different state license plates. I also remember drawing lots of laughs by calling out the street signs in Morse code, dit, dot, dit, etc. We also took ski trips with the church to Monarch Ski Resort in Colorado. Those were wonderful years.

At the time, we had purchased a larger home in Overland Park at 101st Street and Lamar. My mom and dad had moved from Des Moines to Kansas City, where my sister and Debbie and I now lived, which enabled us to see each other on a regular basis.

I was happy, and I believe God was pleased and blessing us, even though sin was crouching at my doorstep.

As lay ministers, Debbie and I arranged outreach events, often for Russian Jewish immigrants. One such event was with Alyosha Ryabinov, an amazing Hebrew Christian pianist, from Kiev, Russia, who played at retirement homes. Alyosha learned to play at a very early age and found the Lord in the most difficult of times for people in that country, by merely reading the Bible, as I had. He is a wonderfully humble man with a gentle quiet spirit. Thank you, Alyosha, for sharing your life with all of us.

The Bible is so true, and all our Messiah Jesus' words are 100% true. Read Luke 11:24–26. When an unclean spirit leaves a man, it says that the spirit goes through dry places seeking rest and finding none, he returns to the house where it came from, finding it swept and put in order. Then, he takes with him seven other spirits more wicked than himself and they enter and dwell there and the last state of that man is worse than the first. I experienced this.

Was I saved? Yes! Had I walked with God? Yes, in some areas. Was I sanctified or set apart as holy for God's service? No! Why? I viewed all spiritual and secular work accomplishments as my own rather than originating as gifts from God. I boasted about them. I was filled with pride. These became idols in my life which God hates. I also lusted continually and committed other unmentionables. In Proverbs 16:18, the Bible says that pride comes before the fall and a haughty spirit before destruction. This was my wilderness experience for many years that followed. Do not follow this path.

Due to my ever increasing pride and unholy life, I had seen God's mercy and grace toward me. The Scripture says in Psalms 145:8 that God is gracious and compassionate. In Lamentations 3:23, it says that His mercies are new every morning, and, in Psalms 136:1, that His mercy endures forever. The Bible also says in Hebrews 13:5 that He will never leave us nor forsake us.

God's mercy toward me has continued throughout the many years that followed along with His discipline.

Big Companies, More Responsibilities with More Stress and My Church Experiences

After losing my job at the City of Olathe, I was fortunate to find work at United Telecom, which later became US Sprint, and I was hired to do financial analysis for every major hardware acquisition. I plotted usage on mainframes using linear regression analysis and determined the useful life of major hardware purchases. I also calculated the payback, net present value, and internal rates of return and wrote and packaged all this data into what was referred to as a "Board Resolution," which was a document submitted to Sprint's Board of Directors for review and approval, often for million dollar acquisitions.

My performance earned me a promotion to US Sprint's first IT Budget Manager. In this capacity, I managed a staff of thirty who prepared Sprint's first IT budget. If I remember correctly, it was about $250,000,000 in the 1980s.

Later, I was promoted to Director of Data Base Technologies, where I managed and hired all the staff as well as analyzed and made recommendations to purchase and support new and existing databases, principally Software AG and DB2. I reported, along with three other Directors—Steve Dubois, Dave Antes, and one other—to Charles Price, the CIO who was also Vice President. The job involved lots of travel to Dallas, Ohio, Los Angeles, and Florida, and the travel took its toll.

Our VP had taken up golf so, when we traveled, we usually played golf during the day and worked at night or went out for drinks. Charles Price was a gentle kind man. I liked playing golf with him, although his game surpassed mine very quickly.

When GTE Sprint and United Telecom merged to form US Sprint, they took controlling interest in the new company and decided to replace much of United Telecom's Information Systems staff. The company needed the merger to fund the building of the first coast-to-coast fiber optic network.

Cliff Hall, Joe Piro, Stewart W., and two others from GTE, replaced all of us Information Systems folks from United. Joe was the hatchet man and also became my boss. I asked to stay, since Debbie and I were entrenched in Kansas City's Christian movements and Messianic Jewish outreach. But, we all suffered because I took a salary cut from $85,000 to $50,000. This was very stressful for a man like me with a wife and three children to support and many other mental and spiritual issues.

During that period, I traveled to Sprint's four data centers managed by Stew W., who was VP of Operations. I taught his staff how to evaluate computer acquisitions. I was also spending a lot on escorts when I traveled. In addition, I had made an inappropriate advance to my secretary and was fired. As the world would say, I worked hard and played hard. No excuses, only regrets. I remember Debbie, tearfully crying when I had to take these trips. I am sure she knew deep in her spirit something was wrong.

When I left Sprint, I sent a letter to Ron LeMay, a former executive from AT&T, then an Executive Officer of Sprint's Legal Department, whom I worked closely with reviewing hardware contracts. I told him how devastating the merger had been on my life. He later became Sprint's President.

As the fiber network came to completion, Sprint purchased the controlling share again and Sprint fired the CIO and his four Vice Presidents, including Stew W.

During those years, I had cohosted a radio program with Dr. Andrew Meyers, a Messianic Jewish General Practitioner, and Dr. Neil Weiner, who had been an Economic Advisor to Richard Nixon prior to his fall.

The three of us discussed issues pertinent to understanding how Jesus fulfilled the Scriptures and is our Jewish Messiah. I can't remember the name of the program or how long it ran. Andy and his wife, Sharon, were good friends with Debbie and me. When I had problems, he was a great counselor.

The above experience was during the era of Chuck Colson, who was sent to prison for his involvement with Watergate, at which time he became a Christian and started Prison Fellowship ministries. I met Chuck on one occasion.

Before the Sprint merger, when I traveled with my colleagues on business trips, I had been on the slide long enough and had become seared in my conscience to the extent that I went along with the party. I was leading a very compromised unholy life.

In addition, I had been committing the unmentionables long enough that I had become very perverse and distorted in my soul and developed a relationship with a hooker named Kim in Kansas City. In my warped mind, I felt sorry for her and her son, who she often took with her. I paid for sex and bought him gifts. She didn't steal but did do D, and that helped squelch my pain and guilt. How could I do this to my wife and children? I was now not just on a slide, but on a roller coaster slide downward, and my life was descending totally out of control. Demons had come back sevenfold in my life. My sins were discovered, and we were separated.

Debbie, God bless her, and a couple of our friends, Terri Kallevig and David Alschultz, who both had Inner City Ministries, helped Kim and her young son. I don't know Kim's ultimate outcome, as I did not know mine, at this time in my life. I was with Kim and her son all night and, when her husband found out, I was in danger whenever I was in her area.

I remember one instance where I had gone to the Kallevig's home to pick up something from Terri. She was babysitting Kim's son. When he saw me, he came running out to meet me, probably expecting a gift. I broke out crying since I realized how much I had ignored my own children's needs while helping Kim's son.

The steep slide had really just begun. I was being disciplined severely. Fear was very prevalent in my life because I knew I was going to be separated from, and can possibly lose, my family. During this time, I began using and committing more unmentionables to ease the pain in my soul.

Prior to this event, Debbie and I had left Full Faith Church of Love to attend Kansas City Fellowship. It was fostering a new prophetic movement led by a man with great zeal, Mike Bickle. I don't believe it was God's will for us to leave Full Faith Church which we had attended for years.

When my sins were revealed, I was asked to make a public apology to the congregation. I did not understand how a public confession to the whole church would relieve the pain I was experiencing and heal any wounds I had created. So, I felt abandoned, rejected and, like so many times before, a failure. Of course, I had hidden my past for years.

I felt that I had lost all my faith. I was the seed planted amongst the thornbushes, which grew up and choked the plant as stated in Matthew 13:7. I was double minded, leading a double life unstable in all my ways, as stated in James 1:8.

Even during this period, we, on one occasion, entertained others at our home, including Lauri Boone Browning, Pat Boone's youngest daughter. Unlike many, I was not personally convinced that the Prophetic movement was really a new major move of God. However, who was I to judge? I was being disciplined by God.

An associate pastor at the time had counseled us and, during this session, he prophesied to me that, if I did not repent, I would go to Canada somewhere and commit suicide. God spared me since I had read enough Scripture producing enough faith in me to never consider that again. The Bible verse is 1Corinthians 3:17 that says, If I destroyed God's temple, my body, God would destroy me. I am really not a risk-taker when it comes to death. Remember Grandma's Christmas article. Later, Mike Bickle, the pastor, asked me to leave the church since Debbie was attending there. My kids at the time were attending their Christian school.

I need to explain another reason I attended Kansas City Fellowship Church. With my low self-esteem, brought on by my own mistakes, as well as my past and former successful friends, before my sin being exposed, I sought association with whomever I could find who was "famous" to make me feel more important.

Of course, this did not work, but I had some interesting encounters. Laurie Boone Browning attended the church with Bill Kenney and Todd Blackledge, co-QBs for the Kansas City Chiefs at the time, along with wide receiver Stephone Paige and another wide receiver, Emile Harry.

Emile Harry became a friend. Emile graduated from Stamford University and, in college, was back up QB for John Elway, later QB for the Broncos. I met Emile at a church picnic. He was a really nice guy, and would throw some footballs to my son David at church picnics. I think he majored or minored in Computer Science, so we were on some common ground. I felt at ease talking to him about my issues, and he invited me to his and Sonja's house to chat. That was relieving to me but did not effect a change in my life. Nevertheless, I was moved by his compassion.

I pretty much gave up at that point and ran from church, God, and the faith God had given me. However, as broken and lonely as I had become, God never left me nor forsook me. He continually had mercy and kept me from total destruction and death for years until I was again able to begin to see His work in my life.

I had fallen deeper into darkness than I ever had been in many areas and did not realize it would be years before restoration began. I had hurt my wife deeply and my children, and spent my hard earned money on D and unmentionables and didn't know what to do. I also betrayed my Christian friends. Understandably, Debbie no longer trusted me.

I lost my family, friends, home, job, and had to move in with my mother. God's discipline was being executed on me. I was very dependent on D and the unmentionables, and was walking around fearing what might be next in my life. I was living a life of lies and alibis. I had become very lonely. Was I the exception? Had I sinned worse than anyone in the world? I felt I had.

Fortunately, God does not look at our failings as we do. After all, He is our Savior before our salvation and our Sanctifier after we are saved. He always has merciful outstretched arms waiting for us to return to Him. In fact, He pursues us, His lost wandering sheep, and protects us from ravenous wolves. Today, I understand more than ever the depths and breadth of His mercy and love toward me and others that may be in some way like me.

My First Consulting Job, Revenge for Me, Discipline Then Mercy for Another

After leaving Sprint, as earlier mentioned, I found a job with MTW Corporation as a consultant. I worked directly for George Mueller, the President. One morning, shortly after the former GTE guys were fired from Sprint, they all showed up at MTW. Were they looking for work? I never knew, but, at the time, I felt that God had executed His discipline on them. They had reaped what they sowed since they had been replaced. Of course, so had I. I later lost my job at MTW due to a lack of work. Who was I to judge another?

Long after Stew W., the former VP of Operations, was terminated from Sprint, due to depression and other issues, he attempted suicide by holding a gun in his mouth and pulling the trigger. It failed. Later, he gave his life to Christ and his story of hope and relief from depression has helped many.

Years later, after Debbie and I were divorced, she attended a conference of Stew's and he recounted working with me at Sprint. I had no knowledge of his attempted suicide. A while back, long after Debbie had forgotten that she had met and shared this story with me, I located Stew on the Internet, now eighty, and we had a wonderful conversation about the Lord and our lives. We also discussed book publishing. What a blessing!

My Dad's Salvation and Death Testimony Never Told

In the1980s, after my slide had begun, my father had a heart attack. He was a heavy smoker at the time but soon, after heart attack number one, he gave it up. I was there for him and rushed him, with Mom in the car, to Kansas City Medical Center where they were able to revive him. This happened two more times. Again, on one of those occasions, I was able to get him to the emergency room where he was given shock treatments to restart his heart. Had he not made it to the hospital, he would have probably died.

My dad's third heart attack was more serious. He was rushed by ambulance to the hospital, where he remained in intensive care. The doctors gave him a 20% chance of survival. Furthermore, in running tests, they discovered he had prostate cancer. Additional tests revealed that the cancer had spread.

They performed a radical prostatectomy and found more cancer and, shortly thereafter, he was released to go home and die.

Before he was released, my sister and I were waiting outside the emergency room discussing which of us would go talk with Dad about Christ and pray with him to be saved. He had always shunned what he referred to as "religious talk." I won the coin toss with my sister, and proceeded to go into the ER, share Christ with Dad, pray with him to repent and ask God to forgive his sins, which he did. Afterward, with a smile on his face, he looked at me and said, "Why didn't I listen to you years ago?"

Dad had problems like I did, but never as severe as far as I know. We never discussed his issues. He was taken home to their apartment in Kansas City along with a rented hospital bed where he remained until he passed away. The night before he went to be with the Lord, I was with him and remember him calling his brother Bill, laughing as they always did, and calling other family members who were still alive. Afterward, as I spoke with him, he looked at me and said, "Who is that standing at the end of my bed?" I saw no one, and later realized it was the angel of death who would lead him on his journey to Heaven.

The next morning, he asked Mom for a drink of water which she brought to him with a straw. She placed it to his mouth and, instead of sucking in the water, he expelled air with his last breath. I miss Dad a bunch. I wish I had more years with him, but I am so grateful that we will be reunited soon. He was a hard worker, took care of Mom and all of us, and helped get me out of many jams.

CHAPTER 3

Discipline with God's Continual Mercy Throughout

Death, Not Life, on the Streets

I WAS SAVED, BUT not sanctified nor set apart from the world for God's work in many areas in my life. I held to a form of godliness, but denied His power to heal and deliver me. I held onto sins I thought were normal from my upbringing. I was stuck in an endless cycle of sin—suffer guilt, repent, and then repeat. I would berate myself then, furiously flip pages of the Bible trying to crack the "victory code." God was judging me as a Christian. My actions became much more wicked but ultimately brought God's serious chastisement along with the breadth and depth of His mercy and grace in my life. It's a dreadful thing to fall into the hands of the living God as it says in Hebrews 10:31.

Strangely, I still read Scripture and prayed in tongues. But, until I came to know God loved me, and would forgive my serious sins as a believer and make my life better, I was destined to wander. In Romans 6:1, the Scripture asks the question, shall we continue in sin that grace may abound? Certainly not! But, how would this cycle cease? I would even bind and cast out demons, which would merely come back to tempt me.

I didn't understand deep repentance. I read Romans 8.1, "There is now no condemnation to them that are in Christ Jesus who do not walk after the flesh, but after the Spirit." I felt condemned since I walked after my flesh in darkness, not following the Spirit. All my attempts to fix the fix that fixed me failed.

During these dark years of my life, God taught me many things. He spared me from dying. He started planting in me a love for everyone regardless of color, nationality, or personal wealth, or whether someone was deeply hurting due to their mistakes or extremely successful. God loves us all, and His sunshine rises on both the wicked and righteous.

My Kansas City Street Life, My Occupation and My Street Name

Kim had introduced me to crack cocaine, a real pain-killer and pain creator as well. At first, it produced euphoria and a numbing effect I had never experienced. It gave me energy, but those highs were short-lived. The more I used, the more paranoid I became and the more D I wanted. The withdrawal left me exhausted.

In the late 1980s, as mentioned, I had lost my family, home, friends, and church. And, I was living with my mom, scamming money from her to buy more D. I was in and out of work and, for a time, used the proceeds from the sale of Debbie and my home on 101st Street to buy D. I partied and used with whomever was available at the moment. D and the unmentionables went together.

I continued to use D, trying new forms, to feel the effects. At some point in my using, I partied with a girl name Nancy who lived off of 77th Street in Overland Park, but always could be found in Kansas City on Main Street. I partied with her a lot, and would even pick her up in the morning before we copped our D. I met her parents; her father owned a gas station on Southwest Boulevard. We talked a lot and, since I was much older, her father must have thought I would protect his daughter. He even asked me to go with their family on a vacation at one point. I declined fortunately. Through Nancy, I learned how to mainline.

Nancy introduced me to some Cubans. Their names were always preceded by their nationality. There was Cuban George, Cuban Francisco, Cuban Tony, Cuban Nelson, and Cuban Ray. I was named Ray and there was an Afro-American named Black Ray, so I was called White Ray. I shiver when I recount this period of my life. They all came from Florida to Kansas City and had originally arrived on boats from Cuba when Castro sent criminals to the United States during that period. Many survived by selling cocaine.

I knew Cuban Tony pretty well. He was actually half-Cuban and half-Italian. I sometimes partied with one of his girls whose name I have forgotten. One evening, I was with one of his girls and he was with another at my new apartment which I had rented from another NA member, who later became an actress in Hollywood. Her name was Val. Tony always had a gun next to him. He was a dealer not a user. That night, I ran out of D and money, and he claimed that he did as well, which is the way a dealer lets you know that you are done for the evening. I withdrew alone. That was my first experience with Cuban Tony.

I am reminded of two events that followed involving Tony. The first involved another girl I used D with who was Tony's girl. She was married and had kids and lived in Shawnee. She had a bad habit of stealing others D. One evening, I was riding with a bounty hunter, a user also, looking for another user, Michelle, who had a warrant for her arrest and had borrowed my car for a few days leaving me stranded. I was with Michelle's mother and her boyfriend, a former preacher whom I knew. Ginger, the bounty hunter, informed me that Tony's girl had gone missing. She was later found dead in a house in east Kansas City, and Cuban Tony was the prime suspect. I was not sure until later about Tony's outcome.

The other experience I had with Cuban Tony was in the upper level of a nice hotel on Main Street, not too far from the Museum of Fine Arts. At this time, I was there for the usual reason, but in the room were quite a few business types like me sitting and discussing business with Tony. Tony pulled his gun and demanded that each come with him to the bathroom. While pointing his gun at our heads, he asked each of us individually if we had purchased anything from a certain person. I, of course, said no and was released. That was my last encounter, fortunately, with him. God's mercy endures forever.

A second episode involved Cuban Nelson. In downtown Kansas City, there was an old hotel at 1111 Grand, today renovated into a luxury hotel, The Ambassador, Kansas City. When out of money, I had given Nelson my second wedding band to hold as collateral for D.

Nancy had introduced me to Nelson; and, Nelson, knowing I was a business type, introduced me to Bill and Chuck. Bill was a businessman and owned a business which received computer shipments from the Far East loaded with D in their compartments. He also owned warehouses in the Kansas City bottoms where we later partied. Chuck was an enforcer who boasted of the guns he had built as a kid. Bill and Chuck were both friendly, jovial guys as long as you stayed on their good side. We hung out a lot together using D as long as I paid.

The old building was a hub for drugs. The first floor was like any business with a receptionist. The second was where Bill had his office and the third was where Nelson cooked his crack in a microwave. It was there that Nelson had held my ring as collateral for a D purchase. The Feds were monitoring this location.

We knew it was hot because we always saw the same vehicle with a driver parked at the end of the street. As a result, Nelson decided that he needed to relocate. I was living in an apartment in Shawnee Mission, so he packed up and moved in with me still holding the ring he had around his neck until I was able to repay him.

I remember Nelson being a pretty nice guy, also keeping his gun close at hand. When he moved in with me, he brought it all with him. I was not just a little worried. He made regular runs from Kansas City to Florida or New York to pick up supplies and myself, along with Bill and Chuck, became sponsors. I remember Nelson lecturing me on the evils of using D and how I could make more money if I did not.

As the heat built on my apartment, he packed up his vehicle with all his possessions and traveled to New York. Somewhere during his trip, he met another friend and, as recounted by Bill, from the newspaper, he was driving along a highway on the East Coast, and was pulled over for speeding by a cop. They had stashed their stuff in the gas tank compartment. They thought they were being busted and opened fire on the police that had stopped them. The police returned fire and wounded Nelson in the stomach and his friend in the leg. That was the last I heard from him. They probably went to jail or were deported.

I had been left a substantial amount of crack to use in his absence which fortunately was flushed by my NA sponsor when I called him for help. This was the world I had fallen into through my sins which started with the unmentionables. God's mercy never ceased. I was not murdered nor did I go to jail, or die of a disease.

One more story involves Bill and Chuck. As mentioned, we hung out together everywhere doing crack, Chuck's house in Raytown, Bill's warehouse in the KC Bottoms. We also hung out in some pretty bad areas east of Troost Avenue in south Kansas City. Chuck and Bill were well-known wherever we went, so everyone, regardless of race, color, or creed welcomed them and myself into their D house.

Chuck was a tough cookie whose wife had been injured in a boat accident (explosion). He once invited myself and a friend to his lake home. He asked me to bring D, which I could not locate. At the home, he had one of his friends. And they asked if I would like to go into the woods and watch him fire one of his prized homemade weapons, an open-faced repeater. I declined, stating I would stay back and watch for intruders.

I also remember him telling me about a friend who, having hocked something for some D east of Troost Avenue, returned to the house where he had made the purchase with a grenade. He pulled the pin, holding it to keep it from firing, and asked for his valuables back. Needless to say, there were no questions asked. Chuck taught me a lot about street life. I thought I had fallen as far as I could, but God had more discipline with mercy to reveal to me.

Strangely, I felt compassion for Chuck and Bill, realizing they were at their core good people having fallen like I had into cocaine corruption. Bill had a wife and, I think, a daughter. Chuck was married and took care of his wife who had been injured in the boating accident and was in a wheelchair. At one point, I convinced Bill to attend a Narcotics Anonymous meeting with me.

They were big guns, but not the biggest. That encounter is in my next story.

NA Does Not Mean I Am Not Accountable

I had been arrested twice in Kansas City for DUI. The first time, I was sent for treatment at a halfway house near Troost Avenue and 30th Street. The second time, I was sent to a treatment facility in Shawnee Mission, Kansas, facing Interstate 35. I attended NA meetings in Kansas City at a group called CAG, and also at another group that met in Merriam, Kansas. I may have been to a third treatment facility, but I don't remember the name.

At the second or third facility, I met Michael Tutera. In fact, I roomed with him and we became good friends. This is how God reveals His wonderful works in my life. When younger, my primary care physician was Dr. Lees Forsythe. His partner, whom I saw occasionally, was Dr. Tutera, Mike's father. Mike's wonderful mother managed a retirement home in South Overland Park off 103rd and Metcalf where my mom had eventually moved after my dad's death. Mike owned the building, and guess what? He also owned the building at 1111 Grand. Mike was trying to get clean, as I was. I remember him unscrewing light bulbs to see if the room we were in had been bugged. I will share two anecdotes about Mike.

Mike lived in Mission Hills, a very expensive area in Kansas City. In fact, he didn't live too far from where Joe Montana resided when he later arrived in Kansas City to play for the Chiefs. When in the treatment facility, Mike told me that, when he got out, he would give me either $1,000 to get my feet back on the ground or $1,000 of D stashed in his safe at home.

After failing to turn my life around in treatment, one night I was partying with a girl and I called Mike to take him up on his offer to give me his stash of cocaine. He said come on by, but bring no one with you; so, several blocks from his house, I had the girl with me get into the trunk until I returned. I arrived and he escorted me upstairs and proceeded to show me his immaculate collection of guns of all types in drawers that looked like a filing cabinet. His wife boasted about one stating, "That's mine." I stayed quite a while and don't remember leaving with anything but, fortunately, the shirt on my back. After returning to my car and driving a few blocks, I let my disappointed hooker friend out of the trunk.

The second episode was when I lived in an apartment near Walnut Street and East 37th Street. I was very messed up and had four guns of my own stashed under my bed: a 38 revolver, an antique 22 revolver, a 410 single shotgun, and a 12-gauge shotgun. Three, I inherited from my father. I had been hosting a girl and her two daughters who had moved in temporarily. She had overstayed her welcome, even though she had other places to go. So, I called Mike. Shortly thereafter he arrived with his bodyguard packing, and ushered them out. No harm done to anyone. Again I received mercy.

As mentioned, I don't get my jollies from sharing these horrific stories, and there are many more; but, I share only so someone who may eventually read this book understands how God pursued me as I wandered as a lost sheep through the woods filled with wolves ready to attack. I also share, so whoever reads this will understand the progression or slide of the unmentionables. Today, I don't fear much because I know God's power to save and keep all of us even more if we trust Him.

When I finally left Kansas City and took a job in Colorado Springs, Mike gave me the $1,000 he promised to help me get back on my feet. God blessed me through Mike.

I pray that my kids will read this entire book in anecdote sequence and realize that the God who loved me through all this, still loves me today with great mercy, also loves them in whatever circumstance they are in or find themselves in down the road.

Death to Some, Life, Grace, and Mercy to Me

I don't know whether Mike Tutera became a Christian. It is not my place to know. I do know he was shot by intruders in his garage in 2008 and died. You can Internet search if interested.

On two other occasions, once with Kim and once in a house in south Kansas City, Missouri, I had guns pointed at me by paranoid dealers. I was never shot and, obviously, not killed; but, I remember others were not so fortunate and lost their lives to D or became casualties living on the street.

When going to the CAG NA group in Kansas City, I met a lot of people, both successfully working the NA program and some not so successfully working the program. I met a Black fellow who was fairly new to the program. After one meeting, I asked him if he wanted to go to Chubby's on Broadway restaurant. We decided on McDonald's and I agreed to buy him a burger since I had a little extra money. He reminded me of a linebacker on the Chiefs. He was big and looked pretty tough.

Anyway, a few weeks later, having not worked the NA program, I went back out and used D. I went to an apartment off 42nd and Main Streets. I went to the second floor to purchase D. The dealer I met there was a Black as well, much smaller framed. He seemed nice enough. Later, he fronted me or advanced me a $20 rock of crack until I returned with cash.

I returned a few days later, but did not have enough money to buy more and repay my debt. He pulled out a baseball bat as I started down the stairs to leave. At that moment, the big guy from NA whom I had taken to McDonald's entered and stood in the gap for me. Needless to say, I would either be out for the count or crippled today if he had not arrived at that moment; I probably would not be telling this story. That is how God protected me time and time again.

It serves no purpose to continue these stories except to say, now I see that God never ever stops pursuing us with the goal to bring us back to Him. If we refuse, inevitably, He has no choice but to let us suffer the ultimate outcome of our sins; but, unlike many fellow Christians, He never gives up. He knows the outcome anyway and the end from the beginning. He only wants us to learn from our mistakes and return to Him for our guidance and help out of the quagmires we create. His love is so much deeper than we can fathom in our natural minds. I want that compassion for others today. That includes everyone regardless of background or color.

The last job I held in Kansas City before leaving was with Argus Health Systems. I had been hired for my experience with the Software AG package Adabas, Natural and Complete. It was located on top of a hill overlooking the KC bottoms where I had partied, and within a block's distance from where Cuban Tony had moved. I was constantly reminded of my fallen state. It was time to move away.

My Escape to Colorado Thanks to Les Lichter, Not Lex Luther

One of the Vice Presidents of Development at Sprint who left around the time of the reorg was Les Lichter. I get tongue twisted at times and say Lex Luther. Perhaps it's just brain fog. Nevertheless, Les was far from Lex as a person. He was always fun to be around when at Sprint. So, when I had managed to get my life stable enough to update my ever-growing résumé of failures, doctored up to appeal to the reader, I located him in Colorado Springs. He had taken a job there and was now CIO for MCI located in a beautiful office adjacent to Garden of the Gods.

He hired me as a DBA (Data Base Administrator) supporting the same software products I had experience with for years. He said, just get yourself out here and you have work. That was the dilemma. I had no money. So, as I mentioned, my first contact was Mike Tutera. I went to his office, a large room somewhere with a single desk in it, and he wrote me a check for $1,000.

However, I needed more, so I asked my cousin Tom, who had recruited me to pledge Sigma Nu years earlier at Kansas University, and he graciously lent me another $1,000, which I did not repay until years later. I repaid him $1,200, but, at that time, I think my reputation outside and inside my immediate family had deteriorated to mincemeat.

Anyway, I packed my car as full as I could with all my remaining belongings and, in the early morning, stopped by another Cuban friend's house and picked up a couple of crack rocks and proceeded on my way. I stopped once somewhere in Kansas to sleep and smoke. I figured, finally, it's over. I have no access anymore. This was in late 1991 or early 1992.

I stayed in a motel for a week until I found an apartment in the south section of Colorado Springs. That was paid for by MCI. I was very grateful for that job but had not yet repented of my waywardness nor seen God in any of my antics or anecdotes.

In the following anecdotes you'll see how God always answered my prayers, but not quite the way I expected.

My First Encounter in Colorado Springs or How I Met My Second Wife

Upon arriving in Colorado Springs, I stopped at a 7-Eleven to get soda and some snacks. Standing in front was a Black dude, and my street smarts said, Hmmm, he is dealing. I stuck one hand out the window with one finger up indicating I wanted to buy a $20 rock. He approached my car and looked like a fairly friendly guy, so he hopped in and took me where we needed to go. He had no qualms with hanging out with a white guy like me as long as I was footing the bill.

His street name was CJ and a pretty friendly guy. He even invited me to his place where he lived alone, so I agreed and we smoked there. I found out he was a former Navy Seal who had fallen prey to the crack habit as I had. He told me about a young Hispanic woman, twenty years my younger, named Becky Chavez, who he could introduce me to and might be interested in a party. He was partying with a friend of hers.

Becky worked at a grocery store so I stopped by, introduced myself, and asked her out. She was very attractive and always sweet to me. In addition, she was living with her brother but looking for a place to live sort of on her own. I had no scruples, so I asked her if she wanted to move in with me at my newly rented apartment. That was the beginning of our very rocky relationship. I was very lonely those days and just wanted friends.

White Ray in Un Mundo Hispano

Becky's *familia* accepted me with open arms. Her mom was a year older than myself and her stepfather was about ten years younger. Her real father lived in Pecos, Texas, where we traveled to visit a few times. He was a chef by trade. We even played golf on one occasion. All her family were so kind and nice. They loved to drink and have family over during holidays, play games outside with the kids and drink beer, lots of beer, more than I could handle. We also frequented bars and I learned to play pool. Becky and I would stay until we wanted to leave to go party with D on our own.

During those years, I met lots of Hispanic people who were all very nice to me. I would fly my kids out to visit and introduced them to Becky and her family when I should have been spending quality time with them alone. I later did to a degree.

Becky's Wonderful Familia

As mentioned, I had been welcomed into Becky's Hispanic family, who always showed me great kindness and love. The family could cook some amazingly wonderful Hispanic food. In addition, her sister had three children, two girls and a younger son, as I did. Her oldest was also named Rachel and had the same smile and bubbly behavior as my daughter Rachel. Becky's mom and I are friends on Facebook today, but don't talk much. Becky and I were engaged but, early on, we had problems and fights when Becky left on her own to party with her girlfriend and didn't return for several days. We eventually had a nasty breakup, and I returned to living alone. I then moved to an area called Austin Bluffs in Colorado Springs.

Prior to the breakup, I had met Becky's neighbor, another nice guy named Nicholas Q. and his girlfriend, Ginger. Nicky had issues as we all do, but that didn't matter to me. How could I judge him? Look at my past. Nicky always seemed available at any time, day and night, to take care of our partying needs. He later started a business which I think was a clothing store, not sure, and I would see him there. He had lots of business smarts.

We also were invited to his wedding to Ginger, a huge affair with a big mariachi band, line dancing and lots of partying. I had never seen such an event. I was a little surprised, however, when a couple of women invitees got into a major fistfight inside the dance hall and, later, someone was shot in the parking lot.

New Life at New Life Church

After our breakup, I was again lonely and desperate for Christian fellowship. I found a church in north Colorado Springs called New Life and began attending every Sunday. The pastor was Ted Haggard. I liked his teaching and they had a great singles group which I joined and, as strange as this sounds, began to lead a small group fellowship. I attended lots of church cookouts, and other events, but never went for counsel to get my D issues addressed nor my obsession with the unmentionables.

One Christian friend's comments from the singles group I have always remembered. I do not remember his name. Anyway, he was in his late twenties and had an incurable heart condition all his life and was told he would probably die before age twenty. He had lived well past that date. I was able to confide in him my problems. He was celibate and offered me encouragement that God could do that in my life as well. I had never heard that before or since from other Christian friends, but it was God gently speaking to me, and I stored it in my heart.

I met some nice women, none really available, but I never approached any in an unholy manner. I only wanted to get back together with Becky. We eventually did and she moved in with me in my new place in Austin Bluffs. We mountain biked together and did the normal things most people do plus what we had always done. Being the sweet person that she was to everyone that she was, including me, she had been trained as a nurse aide and took care of clients during the day and overnight.

Eventually, we got engaged again and got married by a Justice of the Peace in 1995. I had prayed to God that we would get married, and He answered my prayer as He always does to teach me new lessons. Then, guess what? I lost my job at MCI. Becky was not interested in attending New Life since she had been raised as a Jehovah's Witness.

One day, we were sitting in a coffee shop in downtown Colorado Springs looking out a large glass window. All of a sudden, one of my old Messianic Jewish friends Steve Shapiro, who Debbie and I had studied Bible with in Kansas City, strolled past the front of the shop. Steve and Sheila, his wife, had recently moved to Colorado Springs where he was starting a new practice helping dyslexic kids. I was really excited to see him, but I didn't feel the feeling was mutual. Nevertheless, we exchanged hellos, and talked about the church he was attending and departed. He never offered me his number to get together.

We never encountered Steve or Sheila again. At that point, I realized how much damage I caused to others in the body by my deviant behavior and felt even more guilt and remorse.

I Put Becky in Harm's Way

Becky and I decided to go on a trip to visit my mother in Kansas City. Of course, we took a drive down Main Street after shopping in the Plaza area and stopped at an old house where a mailman I once knew had sold me crack. He still lived there and obliged but he had to make a call. We waited, until his dealer arrived. He was the same dealer who had threatened me with a bat over the unpaid $20 debt before leaving Kansas City to go to Colorado.

This was several years from that experience, so I guess he forgot or had other plans. He kept eyeing Becky. Then, he told us he had to make a trip to east Kansas City to get the D, and asked Becky if she wanted to go with him. Like any of us, who have done coke, sometimes the urges overshadow any common sense. Fortunately, we were still in the common sense mode, and I emphatically said, No! I knew the streets and the way they worked. Fortunately, she listened to me; we left without anything and went to do what we intended to do, visit my mother. Had she taken the offer, she may have never returned.

During all this time, I somehow managed to keep my job, as unstable as I was, and draw a paycheck. I, however, would go to the local loan shark establishment and get a front loan at an exorbitant interest rate which had to be repaid when I got my next paycheck. Insanity does not begin to describe my behavior at this time in my life.

Nevertheless, God kept me from the ultimate consequence, death.

Our Move to Vermont and First Nights

This is an amazing anecdote and demonstrates how God brought about an amazing change in both of our lives which resulted in another relocation, this time to Vermont. I was frantically looking for work, and Becky was looking for me in the *Colorado Gazette*. She ran across a job ad for a Consultant with the exact skills I had in software programming in Burlington, Vermont. The pay was great, so I applied the next day, scheduled an interview, and was immediately hired. The only issue was that we had to move to Vermont from Colorado. That was risky for both of us since we were both Midwesterners and my perceptions of the East Coast were not good. In addition, it was only a six-month contract.

She had always been with family in Colorado, but agreed to give that up for us to move to a new location and get a new start. I am sure her mom, realizing this might be good for both of us, encouraged the move. So, we packed our stuff into a U-Haul with her Jeep Wrangler in tow behind. I drove the U-Haul while she drove my red Subaru from Colorado to Vermont over a period of four days.

We arrived in Burlington the day before First Nights, New Year's Eve on the East Coast. Since it was only a six-month contract, I had to perform well to get a better job when this one was finished. We had no access to hard D, so our lives changed somewhat, but D included alcohol which was our downfall.

Burlington is a nice place. It was birthplace of the original Ben & Jerry's ice cream which we visited often, had a great lakeside harbor, and lots of restaurants. It was and is the home base for the University of Vermont and is filled with many college kids. We had sublet a condo for six months located off Kennedy Drive. We brought our mountain bikes and used them often.

We had barely unpacked when First Nights arrived, and we proceeded to a bar to party and dance. As the night rolled on, we drank and drank more until I could barely walk. Becky had sort of a silly smirk smile on her face which I knew was not a good sign. So, after midnight, I thaid wee neeed to glo. Glo I did, stumbling and nearly falling down the flight of stairs to the exit. We searched and searched until we finally found my bright red Subaru.

We didn't live that far away, but I had never navigated Burlington, Vermont, so I got lost and drove somewhere north on Highway 89, about halfway to the Canadian border and, finally, got off the exit at about 2:00 AM near a small town called St. Albans for gas. It was closed, but I proceeded to bang on the door since I saw a light inside, until, suddenly, a patrol car arrived. The police station was only about two blocks away and someone had reported an erratic red vehicle driving up and down the road in front of the gas station.

I was arrested for my second DUI, and put in jail until I was finally able to find a bail bondsman in the morning while Becky waited for me. I had a DUI much earlier in Kansas City which I was able to get expunged. Later, I found a lawyer, was sentenced to take a rehab class, and had my Colorado driver's license revoked. That was a very large problem for me since we lived in Burlington, and I worked in Waterbury some 30 miles yonder. I had to drive, so I did. Thank the good Lord, I did not die that evening.

Ironically, about five months later, I was on my way late to work in Waterbury and I tried to pass a vehicle on the right shoulder when I was hit by a vehicle turning left across the intersection. The individual I hit happened to be a DA for the State of Vermont. The police came and I was given a citation, but that was it. Evidently, record keeping was not as immediate back then and they had not found my DUI since I had had a Colorado license. However, that evening, after returning home from work, a policeman arrived at our door and changed the citation to driving without a valid license.

My contract was almost up for the State of Vermont doing program work which involved linking address and name records and other data from various state agencies like the courts, police, and other institutions, so a common search could be performed. I had done very well, so my plea involved asking for mercy and referring to my stellar work record for the state. I guess they bought it and released me under the condition that I leave the state, which I had fortunately made plans to do. They took my license, and we were on our way to Massachusetts.

This, again, should have been a lesson to me but you know, stupid is as stupid does.

Chelsea, Massachusetts, Here We Come

In Vermont, I had found another consulting job referred to me by a co-consultant at the time at what was then Massachusetts General Hospital. It fit me to a T since it involved Y2K work using the software I had specialized in for years and, of course, wrote papers about at their international SAG conferences in Anaheim, California, years earlier.

We had found an apartment, sight unseen, in an area called Admiral Hill in Chelsea, Massachusetts, a short distance across a short bridge to Charlestown Navy Yard where my office was located. Upon our arrival in Chelsea, again with our U-Haul towing our Jeep Wrangler and my repaired Subaru, another story, not for here, we got lost downtown. Downtown Chelsea was not a nice place. We used to call the area low-rent when referring to these places and this was very low-rent. We bravely stopped one of the many available police officers on the street to help guide us to Admiral Hill, a gated community near downtown. His first words to us were "Why are you here?" before we asked for help. He then directed us to our destination. That was another close call. He never asked for my license.

The apartment was okay, and it was close to my new office at work. At the time, my office was about two blocks from the *USS Constitution*, also referred to as "Old Ironsides," which I thought was very cool.

I had not recognized God's mercy to me in the midst of His disciplines at this point, but I began to see changes in my life. I was married, somewhat happy, was only drinking and not as much as before, and was not doing hard D. I must have still had some mental capacity to work and solve hard problems.

This was also always God's gift to me. I would fight and search to resolve problems as I had sought and searched to find God by reading the Bible years earlier. Becky was happy as long as we didn't move again. Later, we did.

My Ultimate and Final Job before Retiring

During Y2K, I proudly outperformed several of the other four consultants, three who were all let go before Y2K. That left myself, my friend from Vermont and only staff, with other work to perform to do the Y2K conversion. I eventually did much of the work.

Two of the other consultants were an interesting duo. One said he had sleep apnea and was found sleeping at his desk most of the day. The other was a very angry gentleman who boasted that he was famous in that he was the child in the Norman Rockwell painting *The Run Away*. We completed the task with no fallout 12/31/2000 and the other consultant, who had referred me to the job, and myself were hired by what would soon become Partner's Healthcare, Inc. I was offered a starting salary of $85,000, which equaled what I had earned at Sprint before the merger in the 1970s. I was content and now had benefits like health care and retirement.

Becky and I had some good times and some difficult times, usually involving alcohol consumption. I was equally at fault. When Dr. Jekyll ruled, we had peace. When Dr. Hyde ruled, we were in turmoil. In late 1996, we found an apartment in the upper level of a home, so we moved again to Medford, Massachusetts. Becky said this would be the last move for a while and I agreed.

My Son Comes to Live with Me in Medford, Massachusetts

Becky and I had some good and not so good times together. When we studied with a Jehovah's Witness couple and attended their church, things went well. When we drank, things did not go well. I knew enough Bible to retort most of the Jehovah's Witness doctrine and refused to join their church.

Our life was best without any D, and I had no desire for the unmentionables at the time. However, alcohol had caused much stress in my life at home and was affecting my work.

In 1998, Becky and my relationship had hit the bottom, our squabbles had escalated to the point that I initiated a divorce. I had also told Becky, not asked, that my son, who was much younger when Debbie and I were divorced, was coming to live with us. The divorce was easy with no children of our own. I paid for her flight home to Colorado, shipped her belongings afterward, and paid her for her Jeep, which I later sold.

I still felt I loved Becky and her family very much and twice flew to visit her in Colorado and Pecos, Texas. It was her first, and maybe her only, marriage. After that, I never spoke with her again. She passed away in December, 2018.

In the meantime, my son came to live with me and I helped pay for his education, first at Bunker Hill Community College, the school where Robin Williams played Professor Sean Maguire in the movie *Good Will Hunting*.

It was a wonderful time for me to be living with my son. We shared spaghetti dinners together and ate out a bunch, and talked a lot. I was graced with enough patience to hear his grievances for the harm I had caused him and his sisters and that produced some healing in both of us. Still, I was hard to live with, being prone to anger often, and too picky about orderliness and cleanliness. By the way, "cleanliness is next to godliness" is not in the Bible. David decided he wanted to move into the dormitory after he was accepted at the University of Massachusetts in Lowell.

The home we lived in was owned by the Aliberti family and two of the Aliberti brothers, Billy and Rick, lived in basement apartments. Billy and I became friends. He was a Christian and God used him to bring me closer to God again. We attended a little Grace Church in Woburn. We also attended church functions. The pastor was Frank Tamilio. Billy, David, and I took hikes together, ate dinner out, camped, and did other fun activities together.

Those were wonderful years and our close relationship has continued to grow since his college days. God has blessed me with a wonderful son and two wonderful daughters who I am able to love from my heart today with Christ's love.

CHAPTER 4

※

Restoration for His Glory

My Best Friend Jane for the Past Twenty-One Years

In 2000, after my divorce with Becky, my second wife, with my son living with me, I answered a personal ad to meet Jane at Anthony's Pier 4 in Boston.

She was attractive, but more than that, she was from Illinois in the Midwest, and had worked on Y2K, as I had. We bonded immediately and stayed at dinner talking for three to four hours. We met a second time at a steak house in a suburb of Boston. We dated and began traveling together on vacations to Aruba, St. Martin, Las Vegas, Arizona, and the Grand Canyon, and later Hawaii, and Tennessee. We took many trips together to Bar Harbor, Maine, North Conway, New Hampshire, and Cape Cod and even more day trips to Ogunquit, Maine, Western Massachusetts, and other drivable locations. We frequently rode bikes together, ate great meals out, walked and swam in the ocean. We also traveled to Des Moines where she met my entire living family at my mother's eightieth birthday party. I met all her immediate family at a gathering her mother had arranged at a large house in North Carolina. She also attended my fiftieth high school reunion where she met all my friends from my childhood, including the rebels turned doctors, lawyers, pharmacists, and business chiefs.

We have grown very close over the past twenty-one years. I always helped Jane doing yard work in the fall, moving from her house into a condo, and whenever she needed me for a hospital or doctor visit. She has always done the same for me. She has ALWAYS been there for me in a pinch.

She loves nature, hiking, and loves to exercise. She has never done D or the unmentionables. As mentioned, she is well-educated and earned her MBA from Boston University and took the necessary classes to become a Certified Financial Planner, although she had a full-time job in a different field, so she never obtained the piece of paper.

As a single mother, she raised a beautiful daughter who today holds two doctorate degrees and is a professor at Aalborg University in Denmark.

We have religious differences, but her life is like Christ in so many areas. When asked if she wanted to know about my past, she immediately says NO. I think that is the attitude that all of us should have when meeting others. We are called to love not condemn. If she reads this book after I have departed, she will know.

She, somehow, tolerates my mood swings, sometimes anger, and weird sense of humor. We always reconcile after arguments. When people ask me why we are not married, I usually respond that I snore too loud, and that is the reason we live about 50 miles apart in separate homes. We see each other every weekend and, of course, when vacationing. But, in reality, both of us have been married, and we each feel that living apart is best for our relationship.

She also is incredibly resourceful, strong, loves folk music as I do, and is very motivated to succeed in life's endeavors, as I have been. Several years ago, she bought a piece of property with a log house on it, negotiated with a builder to tear it down, and built a new one on-site. She did much of the design herself with an architect.

To dispel critical comments, I am celibate today. I am not filled with fleshly lusts nor perverse thoughts, and I no longer need D or the unmentionables to extinguish my anxiety or depression. He has taught me to love and respect her as He has and does to me.

She is quick to point out my shortcomings. I usually listen to her after I get off my know-it-all, pride bubble. She has met my children and Debbie, my first wife, and we have even had dinner together when in the same town. God sees the good in her as He has in me and does in others and works on all of us to draw us closer to Him. She is reserved and quietly private and usually insists on splitting the bill for everything we do.

The cover of this book is a picture of her hiking which I took around 2005 on a hike in Bar Harbor. Back then, I put a title on it, "His Light at the End of Every Tunnel Revealed," hung it on my wall, never realizing it would become a picture on a book I would write at age seventy-five, but I preserved her anonymity. See how small she is.

The significance of this picture to me is that it demonstrates how God works in all of us. At the time of this writing, I have had all the aforementioned experiences in my life, but she is far ahead of me in many areas in her life experience. Besides, I walk much slower than she does. I still have to enter and walk through the tunnel with wolves, bears, lions, tigers, and alligators ready to chase me if I go into the woods on either side. Well, maybe I exaggerated, forget the gators, but you get the drift. In the meantime, Jane is far ahead of me in many areas and has almost exited the tunnel into the light.

We have many dark tunnels in life, but what I have learned from Jane is that the Lord in His love for all of us, walks with us through all of our dark tunnels and He knows when and how we will arrive at the end. I have also learned that criticizing her or judging her for anything is not my calling. Judge and you shall be disciplined. Trust me, I know. Being kind, gentle, patient, long-suffering, merciful, and loving to her is my calling. It is in no way compromising my faith, rather living what I believe God has shown me is His way of treating us.

Jane, today, I love you with Christ's unselfish love.

My Ice Cold Experience That Started at an Ice Bar in Boston

I worked with quite a few Irish folks at Partners that loved to drink at local Irish pubs. I went along and usually showed up early to make sure I didn't miss out on the fun. This night, we were to meet at an ice bar in Boston. I had never been to an all-ice bar so I was excited and, of course, showed up early. By the time they arrived, I think I had drunk two vodka tonics. We all stayed there for a while before going for dinner at a Mexican restaurant. At dinner, someone ordered a pitcher of margarita, or was it two? It doesn't matter. From there we went to an Irish bar for a few more. Finally, I suggested we go to another Irish bar where a friend of mine, Kenny, who formerly lived down the street from my house in Derry, agreed to meet us.

At that bar, they were playing karaoke and I was really good at Bob Dylan songs. Furthermore, Kenny was buying all of us drinks and shots. When the time to leave arrived, I had lost all sanity, self-control, and equilibrium. I was parked a good four blocks away in a public garage. It would cost a lot of money if I took a cab and left my car there overnight. Kenny asked if I wanted to stay over at his place downtown, but I said I'mmmmm fine. I stumbled to my car. Again, stupid is as stupid does. I got in my car, thought to myself, is this really a good idea, and tried to drive home. I entered the turnpike and drove through the tolls and, as I did, I took a sharp right turn to avoid a car somewhere, and smashed directly into a Jersey barrier.

When these kinds of events occur in my life, my first words are always, "I wonder if I can pound this out with a hammer?" Not so. My car was totaled, I was lucky to be alive, and the police were on their way. I was obviously very inebriated so I went to jail. It was really my fourth DUI, but there was no record left of my first some thirty years earlier. Three DUIs in Massachusetts is a felony and often accompanied with jail time. In addition, with a felony and in jail, I could no longer collect Social Security.

I called Jane with my one call; she called me stupid, which I was, I made bail, and she came to pick me up. She then dropped me off at a hotel where I spent the night to sober up.

I found the best attorney which cost me $13,000. However, my sentence was reduced from a felony to a misdemeanor. I did lose my right to drive in Massachusetts for three months. In addition, I was required to enroll in a month-long, in-house treatment program and attend three months of meetings before I could get my license and driving privileges in Massachusetts back because I needed to drive to work. The State of New Hampshire never revoked my driving privileges.

For three months, I took a commuter bus from New Hampshire to Boston to work, fulfilled all requirements, bought a new car in New Hampshire, and, although I walked around work with my tail between my legs when confronted by coworkers, God had taught me an important lesson. Don't drink and drive. He was really saying to me don't drink.

After that, besides some stern warnings from my best friend, she never brought it up again and we remained best friends.

Isn't that the way the Lord works? He judges our behavior and shows His kindness and mercy to draw us closer to Him.

Circle of Friends

Jane and I especially enjoy attending folk music concerts at local coffee houses. During the past twenty years, we have seen many famous 1960s and 1970s singers and artists at these venues, such as: Peter Yarrow, from Peter, Paul and Mary; Arlo Guthrie, who starred in "Alice's Restaurant"; Judy Collins, and many more. However, the one individual who had the greatest impact on my life was Richie Havens.

Here Comes the Sun or Is It Really Son

Richie was the first to sing at Woodstock in the later 1960s. I remembered his music during that period, but didn't know much about him. Then, one summer in the eighties, when actually attending NA meetings trying to get clean, a group of us heard that he was holding a free concert at the Hallmark's Crown Center in Kansas City. There was a very large grassy area in front of the center where people could sit and listen. When we arrived there were thousands of people attending, perhaps more.

When Richie arrived on stage in his traditional dashiki, a cloak or covering of many colors, perhaps like Joseph wore in the Bible, the air was ecstatic. He played a long time and everyone sang along. He always ended his show with a graceful bow, folding his hands together, as in prayer. He always smiled, and loved his audience.

Years later, around 2010, Richie played at the Circle of Friends in Franklin, Massachusetts. He was, of course, much older but still exuded the grace of God and humility in his concerts. He didn't wear his dashiki, but rather beads of many colors around his neck, perhaps a sign of his many friends over the years or many life experiences blessing people with his music.

He always began his concerts with a lengthy tune up of his guitar and didn't hesitate to stop during his songs if it had even slightly gotten out of tune. I don't know if this was due to his age, or his desire to ensure that his audience would not be distracted by a note out of key. He wanted his audience to focus on the words in his music.

He played much longer than most musicians and, afterward, signed autographs for everyone. A picture of us is included.

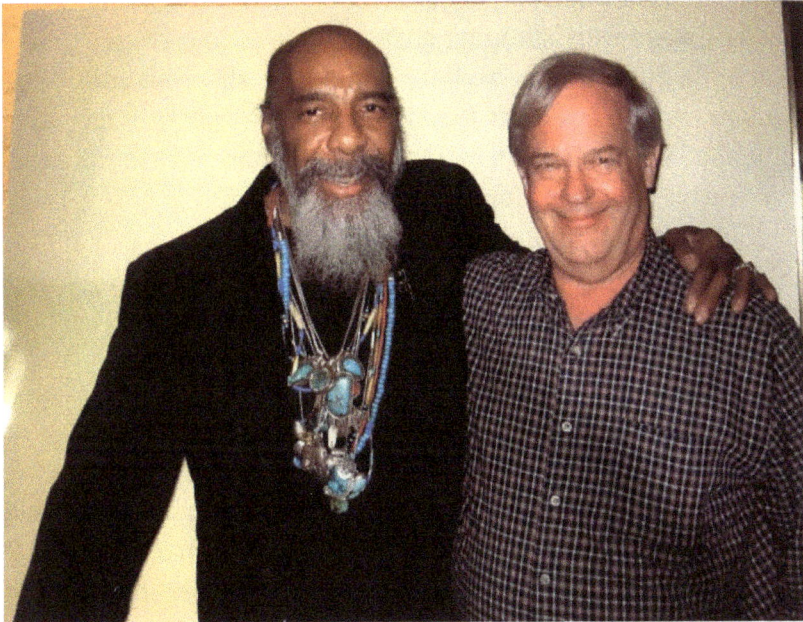

He later signed a poster, **Friends for Life, Richie Havens.**

Richie's music was deep. I still listen to his music and, sometimes, cry with joy. One of his first songs, which he also sang at Woodstock, was a Beatles' tune called *Here Comes the Sun.* I think the message was clear. He did not want to be labeled religious, but spiritual; but, his music and life exhibited God's love for everyone. At least, that was the message to me. He later produced a CD called *By the Grace of the Sun.* Replace the word "sun" with "Son" and his lyrics tell the story.

The last time I saw Richie with Jane was at a musical venue, then located in Londonderry, New Hampshire, about ten minutes from my home. This was around 2012. His music was deeper in meaning and his spirit was very gentle and kind as he rapidly strummed his guitar. I remember his comments at the beginning of his performance, "Isn't it great to wake up in the morning and breathe?" I've never forgotten those words.

During that concert, the power at Tupelo failed and I think a fire alarm went off. Everyone, including Richie, exited the building. Jane and I were standing next to him so we were able to talk to him for quite a while and, for a moment, share his life. What I remember was his great humility. He was a man of fame, who, somehow, kept pride at bay. I treasure that moment in my heart and, today, pray that during my last years on this earth, I will exhibit the Son's humility in my life.

Monk—A Lot like Me

Jane and I also attend various other types of events, like the annual flower show in Boston. I often watched a television show called *Monk*, starring Tony Shalhoub. The show is about a homicide detective who lost his wife in a homicide and, as a result, became extremely anal retentive. He is orderly, and obsessively clean. Everyone chides him, both to his face and behind his back. However, he is the best homicide detective that ever served in the department. He can solve homicides with almost instinctual understanding of the clues and surroundings which his counterparts on the force find incredible. His shows still air on television occasionally.

Jane and I attended an event at Babson College in Needham, Massachusetts. He spoke about his movie career to students and the ups and downs in his life and then opened the floor for questions, mostly to Theater Arts students. I had convinced the person at their box office to allow us to attend the after-presentation meet and greet session, since it was my birthday.

You see, even as a youth, I was obsessively compulsive and would order everything in my room so that if anyone moved anything, I knew someone was into my stuff. I was not as obsessively clean as Monk, but I could sure solve problems that others could not.

We met Tony that night, had a picture taken with him, and, to our surprise, he did not wipe his hands with a handkerchief after shaking ours. He was and, still is, in my mind, a superb actor. I guess sometimes I fit that bill.

Again, God used a famous person in a small way to touch my life and show me how much He loves and cares about me even with my issues.

My Soul and Mind Were Slowly Being Restored

After Y2K, I was hired by Partners HealthCare. My first assignment as a part of a team was to participate in the conversion of the Human Resource Systems, including HR, Payroll, and Benefits from Mass General Hospital's legacy systems to a newer online system called "PeopleSoft." The task was daunting since the legacy system was written in a product called Genesis, which had a great deal of different types of data stored in different formats in different length records. It was not easily extracted into flat files which we needed for the conversion. Furthermore, many of the reporting systems were written using Software AG's product called Adabas and Natural.

I had an advantage, perhaps from my early days at the City of Olathe, since I had great successes writing code using Adabas and Natural. One day, I was asked to attend a meeting with the consultants who had been hired to assist staff with this conversion effort. I knew from prior experience at Olathe that, generally speaking, consulting firms will promise most anything for big money and take years longer than needed to complete the task.

So, during that meeting, I told those in attendance that I could write a utility in Software AG code that would enable every programmer to extract data from the Genesis and Software AG files with very little effort. I was jeered at and perhaps became the laughingstock after the meeting. Besides, this was not my primary charge.

During the next week, I wrote the utility at home during the evening and began using it myself. I passed it onto the other programmers who also used it with amazement at how easily and quickly it enabled them to extract data from the legacy systems. I never got any personal wows or credits for that effort, only that I should not work at home at night. Today, it does not matter, because I see how the Lord was using that to show me that pride in my accomplishments was not as important as helping others.

Following that, I participated in the conversion of about eighteen other hospitals from legacy systems to PeopleSoft as the technology progressed from online systems to Oracle PeopleSoft on the Web. With others, by the time I had retired in January 2018, I had received ten Partners in Excellence awards.

How My Finances Were Restored

After being hired by Partners Healthcare, at age fifty-one, I embarked on a rigorous, debt-reduction program followed by a saving plan. Every year, I saved as much as possible so I would be able to somehow retire at or after age sixty-five. I did retire at age seventy-one. I also gave to an international Christian ministry regularly. The Scripture says in Luke 6:38, "Give and it shall be given back to you, pressed down, shaken together and running over it will be put in your lap." I had learned this years earlier when I walked with the Lord, and as God's Word also states in Isaiah 55:11, "My word that goes forth from My mouth, it will not return to Me void."

Today, almost eighteen years since I bought my home, I am debt-free. I use, but do not carry, credit debt from month to month, and I have less than ten years remaining on my mortgage, which is less than one-third of the value of my home. When God leads me, I give. I tithe and give over and above when I see a need. Sometimes, I give to others who have a legitimate need because I believe what Scripture says, not only that God loves a cheerful giver, but also, in Luke 16:9, it says to use worldly wealth to gain friends for yourselves, so that when it is gone, you will be welcomed into eternal dwellings. I believe all Scripture is given by inspiration of God and is profitable for doctrine, for re-proof, for correction, for instruction in righteousness: That the man of God may be perfect, thoroughly furnished unto all good works (2 Timothy 3:16–17).

I am now retired, not a millionaire, but am comfortable and have all my needs met and am able to help others. That is all that matters to me.

God is so loving and faithful to do everything He says in His Word.

My New Old Home and How I Moved to Derry, New Hampshire

In June 2004, I realized that I was throwing away a lot of mon-ey on rent every month and rents were rising. However, I need-ed a down payment to buy a house and had not saved enough for the purchase. Nevertheless, Jane and I began a search, not in Boston or the outskirts where houses were very expensive, but close to the border in New Hampshire where housing was reasonably priced.

I did pray that God would lead me to the house that He had for me. We enlisted a real estate agent to assist. The first house she showed us is where I live today. It has 1,850 square feet which is more than I needed, but I viewed it as an investment. It also had a pool, which for me was an extra special perk, since I was a lifeguard and competitive swimmer in high school and even in intramural sports in college. It had a huge back deck and space for a small garden. I also figured a way to install a forty-foot radio tower in the backyard. We looked at about eight additional houses, many less expensive, before we returned to this house and put in an offer. God confirmed it to be mine.

Although it was built in 1907, it had been completely renovated with new electric wires, water pipes, and beautiful hardwood floors and woodwork. It has lots of windows and light. I like light, not darkness, today.

Jane loaned me the down payment money which I quickly paid back, and she helped me with virtually all decorations. Her creative imprints are throughout my house. My son, who was now attending UMass in Lowell, helped me replace all the old woodwork and door jams upstairs and most of the rotted deck boards, about 80% of the deck. We made many other improvements. I had the master bedroom and hallway recarpeted.

The special part of all this was not all the awesome features of the house, but the time I was able to spend with my son working together. That was time I had not spent with him in his formative years.

Prostate Cancer's Role in Restoration

In 2008, I was diagnosed with prostate cancer. It is not a rapidly growing cancer, but nevertheless, I had to decide what treatment I would have. The primary options were either to surgically have my prostate removed or undergo radiation therapy. I chose radiation. However, in 2018, it was returning. It had not spread anywhere else, but the effects were evident as you can search the Internet if interested. It affected my sexual abilities.

For me, radiation therapy really only left one other option which was hormone therapy. The side effects are definite and debilitating. I do not believe God wants me to undergo hormone therapy for two reasons. First, it alters your hormones, which stops production of testosterone. You basically become transgender. The same basic drug is used for this purpose. It is not even proven that it greatly extends your life but merely may defer death. Second, I feel better than I have for thirty years. I do everything in my house, including mowing the yard, cooking, and, until recently, clean, shovel or blow snow, plant, maintain and harvest a garden. I walk, ride bicycles with Jane, and do a lot of home maintenance myself.

Why would I want to take hormones? There is no sensible reason. Also, it would have forced me into being celibate. Fortunately, when I came to the cross of Christ and repented of the D and the unmentionables, the Lord offered me the gift of celibacy which I gratefully accepted. That is how I have been restored.

I also have had and been treated for bladder cancer and a melanoma on my back.

Today, I don't fear cancer, and I don't fear death. I believe death in this body is like going on a hike in the valley with a storm brewing and with mountains on all sides. When at the lowest point in the valley, the sun rises and the clouds evaporate and you ascend to be with the Lord. This aligns with Psalm 23's description of death in this body if we know the Lord and He has forgiven our sins.

Quicksand Analogy and How Restoration Worked for Me

God showed me that my struggles throughout life were like falling or stepping into quicksand. The more I struggled, the deeper I sunk. My efforts or works to escape were futile. I called for help, but when I was thrown the rope, I merely struggled more. Finally, after years of struggling, I came to a place where I hung onto the rope tight enough and long enough for God to pull me out of the mess I had created.

I had to come to a place where I learned to trust fully and completely in Him, realizing He would do a much better job at carrying me through life than I would. That is where I am today, and it is so much better than I ever thought it could ever be. The last few years of my life are and will be the best.

Like Job in Job 42:10–17, God restored Job's family and wealth. He continues to do this for me.

There is no fear of death when you know your past is forgiven and your name is written in His Book of Life.

My Children Visit Me

Beginning when I lived in Colorado, I regularly flew my kids out to visit me. For me, these were special times, although, I was far from being away from the D habits I had. I remember Rachel, my oldest, visiting when Becky and I were having difficult times before we were married, but I really didn't spend very much quality time with her. I deeply regretted that later. Besides eating out, we didn't do much but sit by the pool at my apartment. I think we may have visited Seven Falls and driven to Pikes Peak, but I'm not sure.

Later, my second oldest daughter, Rebekah, visited me and we did some fun things together like horseback ride at The Broadmoor Hotel and eat dinner there. The horses were very sure-footed when riding up the steep inclines of the foothills. That was not like me at that point in my life. I think I remember skiing as well at The Broadmoor one winter.

Also, my son visited. He was quite a few years younger so, we attended parties at Becky's sister's familia's home. We played baseball, croquet, and other outdoor sports and ate great Hispanic food.

Much later, after I purchased a home in Derry, I flew all my kids out to visit, sometimes together and sometimes separate. I often took them shopping, especially around Christmas. During the summer, they enjoyed my pool, sunning while we joked and kibitzed about each other and family. Of course, we either BBQed or ate dinners out as well.

I also flew to Kansas City to visit my girls and also to Los Angeles to visit my son David. We enjoyed the same kinds of activities there as well.

The healing and restoration process is a very long one. The hurts are deep. I understand that today. Fortunately, the Lord has not abandoned any of us to suffer forever. I had to forgive myself and others I felt might have wronged me before I could be filled with God's love for my children. That day has arrived.

My First Grandson, Jacob

I flew my oldest daughter's son, Jacob, to visit me on several occasions. When he was in grade school, I remember him having a Flat Stanley project. Flat Stanley was a paper image of Stanley, not sure about the name's significance, which I took to visit various locations in Boston and took pictures to send back to Jacob along with Flat Stanley to show where he had visited. We visited the *USS Constitution*, Old North Church, and several other historic sites. It wasn't like Jacob's real visits which came later.

Later, when Jake visited me in New Hampshire, we would drive around in my car talking to various amateur radio stations in Europe while we drove. I let Jacob communicate and it drew massive numbers of European amateurs who wanted to say hello to Jake.

Jake later became an amateur radio operator himself.

I also built my own computer followed by working with my son David to build his own computer. I think the idea caught on with Jacob, and I encouraged him to do the same, which he did and I offered any assistance I could from New Hampshire to Kansas via phone as well as assist with the cost. However, his computer was built to handle flight simulation which he thoroughly loved. Today, he is an officer in the Air Force, and flies an A-10 Warthog. My daughters are successful in their endeavors, including real estate and high-end jewelry marketing. Rachel loves riding her horse, and Rebekah loves home interior design.

I am grateful to the Lord for the work He has done though Debbie, my former wife, and Rick, her husband, who were there in Kansas City close to them.

Returning to Church

This was one of the most difficult things for me to do after the slide. I guess primarily because I had lost trust in the people in the church. I felt, wrongfully, betrayed in Kansas City. Besides, I never attended church to experience my rebirth, but merely read the Bible. I did read the Bible daily on my HP Jornada Palm Pilot handheld, nearly a chapter or more every day along with breakfast. Since 2004, I have read the Old Testament about three times and the New Testament ten to twelve.

I knew I needed spiritual food, as well as physical food, in order to stay spiritually alive. In John 4:31 and 32, when the disciples urged Jesus, "Rabbi, eat something," Jesus responded to them, "I have food to eat that you know nothing about." Read on. He also states in John 6:63 that, "The words that I speak to you, they are Spirit and they are life."

I also realized that the Bible also states in Hebrews 10:25 that we are not to abandon the assembling of ourselves together as is the manner of some. As a result, in 2019, I began to look for a church, well-grounded in teaching Scripture, versus the latest move of God. I always read, God is the same yesterday, today, and forever, so I felt that I needed to come to know Him by reading and studying His Word, not following the latest new movements.

However, I also wanted to find a larger church where I could go and hide in the corner versus be conspicuously obvious to all. That was not God's plan. I found a local church ten minutes from my house named Abundant Grace Church.

It took me a year of excuses before I could go back to church. But, Sean Theodore, the pastor, loves the word of God and preaches it without compromise. Those attending are humble people and Scripture exhorts us to associate with the humble, not the proud. This has been my home body where I have been increasingly fellowshipping over the past year and a half. Sean's teaching has brought freedom to me in my life in many areas.

The COVID Years, A Blessing to Me

The COVID pandemic has been a tragedy for so many people. I realize that, but it isn't my purpose to discuss that here. Rather, the blessings of social media and, especially, weekly Zoom meetings conducted by a dear friend from my early years as a Christian, who is a Messianic or Jewish believer in Yeshua, Jesus. His name is Bob Mendelsohn and the meetings are weekly Bible studies conducted on Zoom.

We study various books of the Bible. He reads and records his message of the weekly chapter we are studying for about 20 minutes, currently Jeremiah, and then the meeting is opened for questions, comments, rebuttals, and whatever he allows to occur for the remaining 40 minutes.

Bob is the CEO of Jews for Jesus Australia and Asia located in Sydney, Australia. There are about twenty to thirty attendees globally, from Israel to Japan, and the United States. Ironically, and wonderfully, my best friend and fellow Christian, Ace, Bob Merritt, also attends so, although we have not seen each other since about 2005 or 2006 face-to-face, we see each other weekly on Zoom. Ace has graciously offered to edit my book which he has done for others. He is one smart cookie, having graduated from West Point and a beacon of light in my life. I have been able to confide in Bob because he has known me since we lived one block from each other in Des Moines. Furthermore, he was not a rebel like myself.

For a year, I also attended a smaller Zoom meeting from the same location to more intimately study various topics and Scripture. These were called D groups, standing for "discipleship" not drugs. In these meetings, I have come close to people I have never met, living one-third the distance around the world of different cultural backgrounds, but with the same hope I have in our Savior and Lord Yeshua, Jesus the Jewish Messiah.

Bob's teaching and encouragement and recommended readings have changed my life. Thank you, Bob. Your eternal reward will be great.

Social media, like Facebook, has also kept me out of depression since I have found many older Christian friends who were willing to take the risk and accept my friend requests. There are many, which I am very grateful for, but a few I have listed in the acknowledgments.

The Lord could not complete His work of restoration in me without my returning to fellowship with other Christians. I understand that today.

How the Monkey Got Off My Back

The restoration in my life really took place over a long period of time, but was most evident from 2000 to after I met Jane. This is not to say I did not still have issues with D and the unmentionables, which I used to address the stress, depression, and anxiety in my life.

Through a friend's friend, I had access to cocaine which I used less and less as time progressed and I used alone. It caused me stomach issues which I masked as being sick to my stomach. I took earned sick time from work but never lost my job. I also smoked or vaped weed, which helped me relax. Once legalized in Massachusetts, I would travel there from home and spend ridiculous amounts of money for vapes of various flavors and varieties. I used these often during the evenings when watching TV, or pay-per-view movies, or porn I had stored on a USB stick.

When Jane was over, I would go into the bathroom and smoke two or three puffs and return sort of normal. Not really. I was too relaxed and mentally fogged. I also coughed a bunch.

I would tell people I vaped for medical use, but the truth was that marijuana with high THC content was more sexually exciting for me than marijuana with only CBD, which merely reduces pain. I use neither today.

The porn I watched was downloaded on a USB stick which I could plug into my TV and use to get relief.

Since my prostate cancer in 2008 had been treated with radiation, my libido had dwindled and I knew that, eventually, I would be totally impotent, which greatly concerned me. Initially, I took Viagra and then later asked for Caverject, an injectable, which worked very well, even though the cost was $212 for a box of two.

In the past two years, I had returned to church, was involved with Zoom meetings, and have been reintegrated into the Christian community to a degree. I read the Bible every day and would pray to be free from constant temptation and lust for any woman I saw. It was a continual battle. I bound the spirit of lust, cast them out of the house, and they would return as soon as my eyes saw someone attractive. My behavior was much like it had been in my teens, but God was merciful and did not give up on me.

I would take my porn stick, delete all the garbage on it, and repent, and, a few days later, load it back. This continued over and over again until, one day, the Lord granted me faith through His Word and Holy Spirit to completely destroy the stick itself, which I did. He gave me faith to believe that He had something much better for me. After doing that, I had more faith to destroy the $200 box of Caverject. And, finally, I had faith the same day to toss over $1,000 of vapes containing THC.

I had come to the crossroads or cross, and I knew it was the end of the line of choosing my way of medicating my stress and other problems which I had been doing since age twelve.

When I chose to dump the junk, and give myself 100% to the mercy and grace of my Savior, always my Savior but not always my Lord, I experienced His deliverance and awesome presence. It was more powerful than I had experienced years earlier.

In an instant, He removed the wrong desires including the lusts, the fears, the anger at myself, and the guilt. I experienced His awesome peace, love, and a renewed faith which I had never experienced. And I was filled with a deep joy in my heart. My soul had been restored and I began to remember details of my past as He revealed all He had done for me.

I had lost my obsessive-compulsiveness to do things apart from His motivation. Now, I only have one desire, to be close to Him every minute of every day for as long as I have remaining on this earth.

I have begun to place Him ahead of everything else in my life. This period was followed by hours and hours of joyful tears of thanksgiving, realizing I had these problems since a very early age.

Jane saw me crying at times, and I am sure she thought I had stepped over the edge to insanity. I had a few conversations with my daughter Rachel when crying. I think she thought I was dying or losing my mind as well. She said to me later, "Dad, we can talk when we see you in May."

My tears were not tears of sorrow but tears of joy and thanks to God for all He had done for me. I had begun to hear His still small voice as clear as a bell as He revealed to me His work in my life, and His plans for me to write this book.

I began listening to Marty Goetz's music, specifically to his CD entitled *I Call You Friend*. I still worship to this daily in the morning and evening and I still shed tears of joy and thanksgiving as I do.

Prior to my complete freedom and restoration, I had prayed a new prayer from Scripture. I asked the Lord to return me to my first love, Jesus. Then, I read and prayed 2 Peter 1:5–7, which was in itself a positive progression back to knowing Jesus.

The first point in the progression was faith and I was exhorted as Scripture says to give all diligence in faith. The Bible also says in Romans 10:17 that, "Faith comes by hearing, and hearing by the word of God."

The second through the eighth items in the progression I had failed to achieve at all. "Virtue," point number 2, is defined as behavior showing high, moral standards. This was where I had stopped, not able to reach the rest that followed. However, God had not finished His work in me. The Bible says, He who has begun a good work in you is faithful to complete it until the day of Jesus Christ (Philippians 1:6). Following virtue in the progression is to be added knowledge, and then to knowledge, self-control, perseverance, godliness, brotherly kindness, and love all in progression. So, that is what I prayed to receive. Virtue could only be received by repenting or changing my mind about porn, weed, and lust.

I also prayed to know God and for Him to know me. I had seen God do His work in and through my life, but I did not want to chance standing before Him in the future and hear Him say to me, depart from me, I never knew you as it says in Matthew 7:23. Added to this concern, I prayed from the Sermon on the Mount, Matthew 5:8, "Blessed are the Pure in Heart, for they shall see God." I had to give up my lying and be totally gut-wrenchingly honest before God and others. This is my goal in this book. I believe this is one reason God is showing me all His wonderful works in my life. I knew that the Bible says God resists the proud, and gives grace to the humble, so I realized deep honesty was a key to my restoration. Anyway, what could I boast about?

One other factor played an important role in me realizing that I had to let go of lust which began with porn. I realized, from an early age, I almost always looked at a woman's body, before looking into her eyes. My opinions were formed by lust, not the integrity of the person. Media, Hollywood, and scantily dressed people, men and women, feed off this lust. It is DEADLY to our spirits and was to mine.

Finally, now, after most of my life, I can look in a woman's eyes and see the goodness God has created in them. In Matthew 22, the Scripture says that we will be like the angels in Heaven, with no marriage or given in marriage, or adultery, obviously. Another Scripture which opened my eyes to Heaven's ways states in Luke 12:3 that what you have said in the dark, will be heard in the daylight and what you have whispered in the ear in the inner rooms will be proclaimed on the roofs. My personal interpretation of this is that we may not have the freedom in Heaven to think and not be heard by others. All being said, it was my time to clean up my thoughts.

Most recently, as I was writing this book, I thought, how in-complete the stories of David, Moses, Jonah, and all the rest who had made major mistakes, would be if their mistakes were left out of Scripture. Pride and boasting would be all that would be left, no humility.

Finally, the monkey was off my back. How wonderful and awesome are God's ways or restoration. Since the day I chose to destroy porn and D, God has opened my eyes to see His work in each of the anecdotes mentioned. More follow, and some are truly miraculous. I am NOT the exception.

I know the Lord speaks to me directly in His still small voice. However, He also speaks and has spoken to me through circumstances or anecdotes in my life. He uses material things and, especially, other people, both Christian and non-Christian, because He is doing His work in everyone, not just me. All we need do is ask, seek, and find and open our hearts and minds to hear Him and see His work in each of us.

God Reveals His Life in Me with Restoration Greater Than at First

My life, God's life in me, has become a small piece of His awesome autobiography.

God's unrelenting kindness brought me to that place of deep repentance. Some Christians had abandoned me, but God never did. His mercy to me endured through all this. Before all this, I was proud of my accomplishments and probably still am, but now I seek to give all the credit for my knowledge to God.

I thought I was pretty accomplished but, actually, I was very lonely, fearful, and insecure having not followed the Lord for so many years. Through all this, God had implanted in me compassion for the hurting people in all walks of life, all skin colors, and all nationalities, not just the white, rich, or famous folks.

Return to Ham Radio on 9/11/2001

When I was hired by Partners Healthcare in 2000, I had a coworker named Adriane. We did not always get along, but we managed our differences and were congenial. On September 11, 2001, at work with Adriane, I was discussing being single and living alone. We talked about activities that kept each of us happy. She liked knitting and, I said, I once was an amateur radio operator back prior to being married to my first wife, Debbie. She said she had a relative, I believe an uncle, that was a ham amateur radio operator.

It was that point the bells went off. I decided to get relicensed after over thirty years, buy the equipment and antennas, and start operating. At the time, I rented the top floor of a home in

Medford, but I proceeded to do what I had to do, and within six months, I was a ham again. When my son decided to live in the dorm at UMass Lowell, I used his room to string a wire antenna. Surprisingly, I spoke to a gentleman in Syria.

My Strong Radio Tower

Later, after purchasing a house in Derry, New Hampshire, I decided to build a tower. I purchased a used tower from a ham in New Jersey.

I rented a truck and Jane and I drove to New Jersey to pick it up. When home, she helped me unload it. It was aluminum so, it didn't break my back. I dug a 3 feet by 3 feet by 4 feet hole in a precise location in my back to anchor the antenna's base. I installed it in such a way that I could lower the tower myself and not hit the house or my deck or land in my pool. My lot is only 100 feet by 100 feet and the tower was 48 feet at its peak.

My neighbor Brendt owns a concrete company called Cellar Dwellers, and he installed the steel concrete reinforcement re-bar, and poured the concrete which has 3–1 inch bolts extended out of the concrete to anchor the tower base. The tower came in three sections and was called a "crank up," with each fitting inside the other. It was supposed to be self-supporting, not requiring guy-wires.

Nevertheless, a few years later, a high windstorm caused my tower to fall down. It landed conveniently on my 20 feet by 30 feet pool cover, not damaging my house, the neighbor's condos, my deck, or me.

Not giving up as I never seem to do, I purchased another tower from a fellow ham who lived in Framingham, Massachusetts. Jane, again, helped me pick it up and bring it to my home. It was called a "tilt over" with the hinged base and a 4 feet long 1.25-inch threaded rod which I could unscrew from its base to lower the tower across my deck and over my pool in order to install the antennas.

I don't climb mountains, trees, or houses. Heights give me vertigo. And, I don't climb radio towers.

This time, I had attached three guy-wires to the tower and made sure they were securely anchored. That tower has lasted me fifteen years and still is fine today.

What is the metaphor of all this in my life? Proverbs 18:10 states, "The name of the Lord is a strong tower, the righteous run into it and are safe." The first tower was insecure like my life after salvation. I had not guyed or strengthened my life with faith in Scripture and a deep trust in God.

My life is much different today. The Lord has strengthened my life so that I know I will never return to its unstable state, depending on drugs and sex to relieve stress and depression. Yeshua, Jesus in His great mercy and grace, has done this for me. My tower.

I loved the beauty of speaking with strangers everywhere in the world through amateur radio, and I started to try to work as many entities, countries, and islands defined by the Amateur Radio Relay League as I could. It was a challenge to me and I loved challenges. To date, since 2001, I have worked every entity in the world except five. That five includes North Korea and four very remote islands.

But, the main goal God was showing me was the diversity and beauty of His people everywhere, both Jewish and Gentile, rich and poor, and of any skin color.

One of my favorite quotes comes from Manhattan Pete, the Italian chef in the movie, *The Muppets Take Manhattan*. Pete says, "Peoples is Peoples, all over the world." I still think about that statement and how I often looked at one person differently than another and criticized or discriminated against one and not another based on physical criteria. I included a picture of a collector's plate from UNICEF which is titled **"The Earth Is But One Country"** from my living room wall. I've had this for at least twenty-five years but its significance is far greater to me today.

Realizing we are all here on earth for a very short time, each having our own failures and victories while being deeply loved by a compassionate, merciful, forgiving God full of grace, I had to modify my old ways of thinking and my actions that followed.

My primary goal today is to be kind and to love every person I meet as God loves them.

I remember that day since it was 9/11, and I remember Adriane because God used her to spring me into action reaching out to the world.

How I Met My Best Russian Jewish Friend

The recent attack on Ukraine by Russia has cemented this anecdote further in my consciousness.

After being hired by Partners in 2000, I met and began working with a Russian Jewish immigrant by the name of Lilya. She was actually from Moldova, formerly a Russian state. She was very friendly and we frequently worked on the same projects together.

After working together for at least two, possibly three years, we were talking and I told her I was born and raised in Des Moines, Iowa. Her eyes perked up, and she said she was from Des Moines after she was brought to America by a Jewish family by the name of Badower.

I think I fell off my chair. See, I lived on 52nd Street, and my friend Ace lived half a block away when my dad decided to sell our house and build a new house at the end of the block. We sold our house to the Badower family who sponsored her and her family coming to the United States. Des Moines had a population of over 250,000 people and I was working in Boston, a long way from Des Moines. This was no coincidence, and I knew God was, once again, revealing His love to me.

Our friendship grew and Lilya told me about her life in Russia during the 1960s. Two families with children lived in a single-flat

apartment with one kitchen and one bathroom and two bed-
rooms. Food was scarce and work was brutal. If you were late
for work once, I think she said, you were given a stern warning. The second time this occurred, you were sent to Siberia as
punishment.

One Christmas, Lilya gave me a Russian *matryoshka* doll.
Mine is actually four brightly painted wooden dolls. Each one
can be screwed open in the middle and fits inside the next larger
doll. So, when they are all put together properly, only one doll
remains. Isn't that a wonderful metaphor of who we are and have
become? We are like those dolls, and our lives are really a com-
posite of others. Some have lesser impacts on our lives and some
have a greater impact on us.

I remember these stories as I pray for the people in Ukraine.
In addition, I sympathize with all who are suffering so much in
the Russo-Ukranian War.

My Pillow

I love all the beautiful colors of the rainbow. I appreciate flowers today. The fact is that without the beauty of God's wonderful colorful creation, things would be very drab, like the movie *Pleasantville*. The Bible speaks about the lilies of the field and how glorious they are and states how much more glorious we are to Him. I have included some awesome pictures, one of flowers in nature and one of pebbles on a beach in the early morning, demonstrating the beauty in God's creation.

"Cape Cod Roses"

I think I own at least one of every color shirt that Polo has ever made, because I appreciate different colors so much. I call these my shirts of many colors.

Soon after I married Debbie in the 1970s, I decided I would take up needlepoint. I did it only once and, at the time, I did not know why I was doing it. Today I do. I stayed up nearly half the night, as I often did, due to my obsessive-compulsive behavior, until I finished the needlepoint several months later. My son has it today, fifty years later, but I have included a picture of it below.

Like the four chapters of my life, the pillow contains four quadrants. It is a pillow of many colors like Joseph's robe. Each quadrant contains many colors woven together to form the symmetrical designs. It represents my life from God's viewpoint and to Him it is beautiful and, now, to me as well. The weaving and different colors represent His work in me, and it is amazing. I am no exception.

I Am the Prodigal and I Wear the Ring the Father Gave to Me upon My Return

The Prodigal Son as written in Luke 15:11–32 is the story of a son who asked for a share of his father's estate. His father granted him his wish, and gave him and his brother equal shares of their inheritance. Then it says, the younger son, like me, gathered all he had, went to a distant country and squandered his wealth on wild living. A severe famine ensued throughout the entire country so he found a job working for a farmer who sent him into his fields to feed his pigs. He was so hungry that he desired to eat the pods he was feeding to the pigs.

He came to his senses one day and thought of how his father's hired servants had food to spare while he was starving to death. He decided to return to his father and tell him, "Father I have sinned against Heaven and you." With humility, he said, "I am not worthy to be called your son. Make me like one of your hired servants."

It says, when he was far away, his father had compassion on him and ran to him, threw his arms around him, and kissed him. The son said to his father what he planned on saying, but his father said to his servants, bring the best robe and he put it on him. He put a ring on his finger and sandals on his feet and said this son of mine was dead and is alive again, he was lost and is found, so they began to celebrate.

This was me to a T. It says later that his older brother was indignant because he had not been treated as well as his younger brother who had squandered his father's property on prostitutes. However, that is not part of my story.

The Lord always rejoices when we fully return to Him in humility seeking His forgiveness.

In the 1990s, I purchased a ring in Santa Fe, New Mexico, when married to Becky. I liked it because . . . it has many colors.

I bought it, but never wore it for almost thirty years. About three months ago, I polished it with silver cleaner. I was not sure of the reason but, just yesterday, the Lord spoke to me and said wear that ring as a symbol of all that I have done for you. Praise God, for being so full of mercy and compassion towards me, His prodigal son.

Why Did I Join Ancestry.com and the Results?

For years, my self-esteem had been very low. It was not based upon what God thought of me, but based upon my own failures, what I had done, and how I looked at myself. Besides, I remember my dad, jokingly stating that we had horse thieves in our lineage. Even on my mother's side, I was told that Eldred, my grandmother's husband's name, was a descendent of King Ethelred the Unready, an early King of England. This was not a favorable line and, fortunately, I have never been able to prove it. I do know Grandma was divorced due to her husband becoming an alcoholic. I never knew much more about William Eldred, my grandfather, and never met him. Also, I actually thought I was a mistake.

As a result, in 2016, I joined Ancestry; and, from a partial tree built by the daughter of one of my cousins, I extended the tree. I fully realized that for every two grandparents, you have 2! (factorial) for each generation back. I never do anything half-baked. I basically dig until I am unable to dig anymore. What I found and was verified was amazing to me. I discovered that William Brewster, the Christian Puritan leader of the Pilgrim colonies, as well as his son Love Brewster, were both passengers on the *Mayflower* and my ninth and tenth great-grandparents. This was later verified by genealogists at the Mayflower Society and the William Brewster Society in Plymouth, Massachusetts. I shared this with other family members and several have been surprised as well.

What I found which has not been verified was also amazing. One Brewster relative married a Witter, and that line led to the Morgan line, specifically James Morgan, the elder of three brothers, the youngest being Miles Morgan, ancestor of JP Morgan. I followed this line using other recorded lineages all the way back to a Welsh king by the name of Siluria Bran born in 43 BC. This lineage included multiple Welsh kings, two Roman emperors, and more. Another line, called the Wheeler line, led me back to multiple English knights, one which was called the Knight of the Holy Sepulcher and another knighted by King Henry VII after a decisive battle during the War of Roses.

I found all of this to be fascinating. Maybe I did have some good blood in me. However, did those undocumented lineages really matter? I am a child of the King of Kings, and the Lord of Lords.

I confirmed, at least generally, that my ancestry was correct when I had my DNA tested. It revealed that I was 48% from Great Britain, 25% from Ireland, Scotland, and Wales, 12% European Jewish, 7% from the Iberian Peninsula, 4% from Scandinavia, and 1% and less from other parts of the world.

The documented ancestor, William Brewster, did matter to me, since he represented God's Christian work through a natural ancestor of my family. I have read at least four books about his life to glean what I could find about him to follow in my own life. On the following page is a picture of my ancestry to William Brewster of the *Mayflower*.

In short, Brewster was educated in both Greek and Latin at Cambridge University. He later worked for William Davison, then Secretary of State under Queen Elizabeth. He later worked for his father who was postmaster and maintained Scrooby Manor. He was instrumental, along with Richard Clyfton, in establishing a separatist church in England. He became the church Elder. The English monarchy did not approve of the separatist beliefs so, eventually, to avoid prosecution and persecution, he moved to Leiden, Holland.

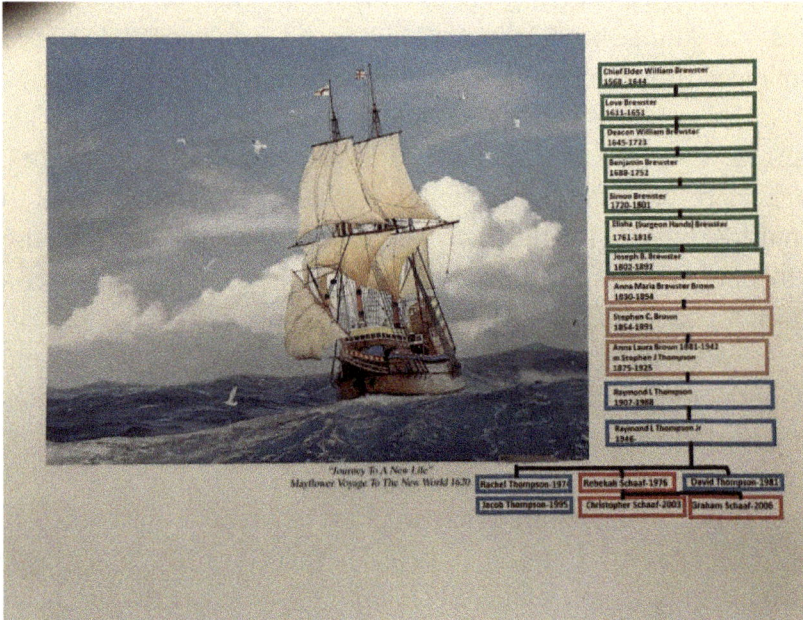

In Holland, Brewster worked with two others and began working a printing press and publishing religious books and pamphlets that were illegally brought into England. The English pursued him through Holland officials and eventually arrested his partners. He went into hiding for two years. The Leiden church decided to send the first wave of settlers to establish a colony in what became known as New England and Brewster went with them. Being the most educated and having been an Elder and taught at the University of Leiden, he was elected as the ruling Elder of the Plymouth Colony. John Robinson, the pastor from the Leiden church, stayed behind. As ruling elder, he performed a major role in the civil and religious affairs of the colony. He also was one of the signers of the Mayflower Compact, a precursor to our Constitution, which defines America as a free nation today.

In about April 18, 1644, at about seventy-seven years of age Brewster died. Governor William Bradford wrote about him as "a man who had done and suffered much for the Lord Jesus and the gospel's sake."

He was someone who was imprisoned for his faith, spent months in the open sea traveling by a small ship to the New World cramped in the lower deck quarters with only beer or grog to drink, saw half of the passengers who arrived in Plymouth die in the first year, made peace with the native Indians and even celebrated the first Thanksgiving with them, and he survived numerous other encounters with Indians, disease, and lack of food, deadly to many. He died, living a full life, being highly respected by almost everyone.

He was the blood example who I wanted to follow in my life. He suffered much but remained faithful. He was a gentle man, kind and considerate of others' feelings.

I sometimes ask myself, if I had not fallen as I had, would I even had these many experiences here in New England, Kansas City, or Colorado and how would I view other people today? God has a plan for all of us. He knows the end from the beginning. It is never too late for Him, as long as we can still breathe, to turn back to Him. I am no exception.

My Kind Italian Barber

I love people of every variety. I love meeting new people. I often embarrass Jane, although she seems to be coming out of her shell, when I strike up conversations with strangers.

One such person, who I love and can talk to anytime, is my Italian barber for the past seventeen years. Horacio is a kind, gentle, and friendly man. We talk about each other's lives and Christ openly. He owns a small barber shop and, usually, no one is there when I get my haircut. He always asks, how I have been, how Jane is and how my kids are doing, how is my health, as well as how my house is, what I have been doing to keep busy, how is my garden, etc. I return the favor and ask him the same. We exchange ideas.

One afternoon, we were discussing death, not my favorite subject, and Horacio told me about his grandmother's death. He was there when she passed on to be with the Lord. I remember his account of her praising God in what voice she had left with her feeble hands raised until she drew her last breath. I thought to myself, I want to be like that lady. This played a role in God's restoration in my life and my view of death. Isn't the Lord wonderful?

The Buppy Anecdote

I love people of all walks in life and sometimes find opportunities in strange places.Jane and I take walks in a beautiful area in Ogunquit, Maine, called Marginal Way. It has breathtaking scenery of the ocean, cliffs, rocks, and especially flowers.Several years ago, we were walking down the street towards Marginal Way and saw an older gentleman working in his flower garden in front of his gift shop. We stopped and introduced ourselves and complimented him on his beautiful flowers. He offered us one. I said thank you, but I did not have a vase.No, he said, eat it. Quite different, so Jane and I did.When I was born, I was given a nickname, Buppy. It was derived from Buster, like Buster Brown shoes, since I was a plump little baby. Another reason and perhaps excuse I use for not being able to lose weight. As I grew, I could only pronounce it as Bupper and eventually it became Buppy. Oh, I almost forgot, since my early childhood friends always called me by my nickname, it was a wonderful boost to my self-esteem.Well, two years ago, we stopped again to look at his flowers and, enthralled, we saw the picture in this book, "Buppy's Bee Garden."

In seventy-five years of life, I've never met another person with the same nickname. We became friends ever since and kept in contact. I learned, later, that Gordon Lewis (Buppy), now retired, was a golf course architect and had designed nearly fifty courses in the State of Florida alone. If I am not mistaken, he has designed around eighty nationally. Google his name to read about him. What a superbly friendly guy.It was special to me because I learned that he grew up in Kansas, where I spent my good years before the slide. In addition, my brother was an avid golfer, and even coached golf for a few seasons at Drake University during his life. My brother Bill also loved people and made friends with everyone whenever he had the opportunity.

Sol, My Creative Helper

Recently, I came to the realization that I no longer liked to clean my house. Bending and scrubbing the tub and properly cleaning the wood floors in my house were painful sometimes, so I just didn't do it as often as needed. Upon Jane's suggestion, I decided to hire someone to help me.

I did a search in my area for those to help me clean and found a young lady with a nearly perfect five-star rating. Her name is Sol. She still cleans for me, so I am being cautious to maintain anonymity. She is from South America and came to this country seeking asylum. She only speaks her language, and I don't, so we use translators on each of our phones to communicate. She is a very attractive woman both in her heart and externally, but I have come to the point where I see her inner qualities ahead of her good looks.

She does her work with impeccable detail. She always smiles and she sings while she works, in her native tongue, of course. She is an artist as well. She makes flowers from paper towels and toilet paper which she leaves near the rollers. She folds everything neatly and places towels and floor mats where I would have never thought appropriate, but which makes more sense than I would have ever expected. She bought me a Christmas gift and even brought some food from her native country for me to try.

We often spend time just translating so I can learn more about her. What a story! A lot of people have difficulties in their life, but how they handle them and how they become filled with so much deep love and compassion, is amazing to me. She is one of those people. I cherish the fact that she is not just my house cleaning helper but also a friend today. Thank you, Sol, for all you are and all you do. Sol has taught me the importance of seeing beyond the physical appearance of a person. She is beautiful in every way.

Shop or Not to Shop, That Is the Question

I have to admit, I like to shop with Jane. When I shop alone, I conquer the store in less than five minutes, only going where I need to and attempting to escape without an empty wallet. Jane, on the other hand, usually covers every aisle in the store, sometimes twice, wearing me out, so I sit down in one of the "old man" chairs to rest.

Actually, I enjoy sitting in the "old man" chairs, not because they provide rest to my aching back, but because I know that someone, eventually, will stroll by and say, "You look comfortable." That always happens and provides a wonderful opportunity for me to meet a new person. The variety of people we encounter in this wonderful life is amazing, and God sees this and wants us to as well. He loves His creation deeply. Remember the example above of the lilies of the field? I want that love for everyone always, even when someone does not like me. Read and pray Matthew 5:43–48.

My Fiftieth High School Reunion and My New Name, "The Reunionator"

I have been given a gift from the Lord which enables me to bring people together from different walks of life. One such example was the uniting of Art Katz with Pat Robertson's son, Tim, to telecast a Passover Seder dinner on *The 700 Club*. Also, I always seemed to unite my rebel friends together as a youth.

When my fiftieth reunion from high school arrived, I decided to attempt to locate all twelve of my former rebel friends, now doctors, lawyers, and Indian chiefs, so we could have a prereunion gathering. It worked and was amazing.

We all had grown old. I better qualify that. We all had grown older, and most of us had become more mature. Most everyone was married, but I brought my best friend Jane, who really enjoyed the old stories and meeting my old friends. It was wonderful.

Ace, the boldest amongst us, asked everyone if they knew Jesus Christ as their personal Savior and offered a prayer to anyone willing. The whole reunion was spectacular. I was reunited after years with my friends from high school, junior high school, grade school at Greenwood Elementary Academy, and even preschool. I especially appreciated seeing my two friends, Mary and Kate Parker (now married) who I had vacationed with at an early age.

I admit, I was an old, slobbery, cry baby upon that encounter which helped me realize that there may still be some softness left in my stony heart.

Lessons from My Vegetable Garden, Cooking, and Baking

Gardening, as in vegetable gardening, is something I loved doing back in the 1970s when I purchased my first home. Jane kept encouraging me to plant a vegetable garden under my ham radio tower beyond my 20 feet back deck in a space about 20 feet by 20 feet and not square. Finally, in about 2010, I had made enough excuses and dug a section of about 15 feet x 8 feet x 12 feet x 6 feet. It wasn't a square or a triangle, or a rectangle, but sort of a plot of land which had no semblance to anything where rows are planted equally spaced apart.

Nevertheless, I planted peas, potatoes, tomatoes, a couple of corn stalks, squash, and cantaloupe. Most did not survive the first season, except for the peas, potatoes, and tomatoes.

The corn was more the size you put in a salad and the rest were stolen by a local thief. I would see him in the early morning brazenly stalking my plants and stealing everything. I now understand the dilemma Bill Murray had in **Caddy Shack**. It was not **Groundhog Day**, it was "Ground Hog Hay Day."

The next year, I decided to put in a fence. Having failed to stop Mr. Groundhog, the next year I put in a second fence behind the first fence. Needless to say, climbing into the garden to plant or pick the only remaining crops I dared to grow, peas, potatoes, and tomatoes, was more risky than climbing my tower . . . in many ways. Jane has insisted, especially at my tender age, that I put in a gate this year. I must listen to her advice, since she is usually right.

What I have noticed is that, each year, I seem to reap a larger harvest than the prior years. Is this another metaphor in my life? I think so.

I always split my harvest with Jane, knowing that she is my assistant and also gives me great recipes, like potatoes au gratin.

As for cooking, as a man, and of necessity living alone, I have learned to cook good food and eat pretty healthy. There is an exception during the holidays, since I like sweets and Jane loves pumpkin pie at Thanksgiving and cherry pie at Christmas, I like Christmas cookies, oh, and oatmeal and blueberry bread. So, big Buppy puts on his baker's hat during the holidays.

What I see today is these talents were given to me by the Lord to share with others. End of this story.

Dieting, Not My Thing

I have tried it all from low-carb diets to weight watchers with weekly meetings. They all consume lots of time and even more money. The results are always temporary.

I lose weight, then gain it back; then lose it, then gain it back. This is much like my other struggles in life.

The only time I had ever been able to lose weight and keep it off was when I was first saved and so close to God that munching regularly was way down in my list of priorities. I didn't have the desire to binge eat or even eat junk food. Maybe food could be compared to an idol in my life.

Since my experience of getting free from the unmentionables and, recently, from D, I have noticed my weight dropping. My priority to eat is less and less. Perhaps the Bible verse in John 4:32 applies to dieting. I have food to eat of which you do not know.

Raymond Thompson Voice Talent, LLC

After retiring from Partners Healthcare in 2018, I decided to try something different. I was told by some friends that I had a really good voice, so I enrolled in an evening class taught by a company called Such A Voice. I was tested along with other classmates and, later, was told by the instructor, who had written a jingle for the old show "What's My Line," that I had an amazing voice. Compliments like this were rare for me and this one went straight to my head. Of course, he may have seen an opportunity to sign me up and make quite a few bucks. So, I proceeded and, for the next few years or so, attended many training classes on voice-overs as well as how to market your voice.

Being more technical and financial, I proceeded to set up my own business and LLC through Legal Zoom. I bought a good microphone, computer software, and hardware and applied for a bunch of voice-over gigs by submitting sample recordings on various web platforms for different ads. I never did cold calls and really didn't have a potential client list of friends to call.

I even had a business account opened where people could click on my web page and it would take their credit card and deposit it in my account. I never used that except for one time, for another event which was unrelated to my business.

However, I learned quite a bit about the business and voice recording. I detest traditional advertising which inundates our lives daily through television, the Internet, and every other form of media. I did have some thought of possibly doing audio voice-overs for books. But, in 2020, I decided to go belly up and discontinue my attempts as a business.

At seventy-five, I am not sure that I can still effectively record, but I still think God may have a purpose for it. I know my first cousin and many others have difficulty reading a book due to cataracts or other eye issues.

Once my story is finished, I will see whether or not I can squeak enough to intelligibly voice-over my own writing.

The Movie *Contact*

Recently, after a long day of writing, I turned on my TV and noticed, for the twentieth time in the past year, that one of my favorite movies was showing. It is called *Contact* and stars Jodi Foster, one of my favorite female actresses. The movie begins with her and her dad operating his ham radio and making contact with a station in another state. This was right up my alley and, since it involved a father and daughter relationship, it always touches my heart when I see it.

In short, her father, who she is very close to, dies of a heart attack, and she proceeds to go to school at MIT, graduates magna cum laude, and then oversees the search for signals from space received by giant radio telescopes located in the desert. Finally, a signal is received which is interpreted to be generated by intelligent life.

I am leaving a lot out, but in a nutshell, the signals are eventually decoded into the plans for a weird interstellar craft enabling someone to travel to the star Vega. Jodi Foster, Dr. Ellie Arroway, is selected to travel to Vega. Before her journey begins, she does not believe in God, but she has met and fallen in love with Palmer Ross, played by Matthew McConaughey. He writes about science and is portrayed as a believer in God.

Upon arrival at Vega, she is reunited with her father, who inspired her eventual career when she was a child. This is a tearful moment in the movie. When she returns, no one believes what she had experienced, except Palmer Ross.

If you overlook all the weird quirky portrayals, maybe not all that weird, of religious fanaticism, you can gain some possible insight into how we think and process our spiritual encounters in life.

The movie makes me think more deeply about what our universe might be like. I have read about string theory and multiverse concepts. Einstein's theory of relativity was balked at for years until proven in the 1920s through light refraction observed in space when passing by a distant stellar object. However, answers always bring many more questions. We, as finite humans, naturally seek for answers to our problems. Why do we avoid the obvious Book of Life which has all the answers we humans need? Do we need to know every physical detail of our universe? Or, can we accept the truth God has already given us in His instruction manual, the Bible, by faith?

Maybe, when Jesus healed a sick person, God changed, at that moment, everything to a different string or universe, one of an infinite number of multiverses. We perceive the cosmos and all that it contains from our space and time perspective. However, God can see all, including the end from the beginning.

Consider that, without a space and time continuum, he knows the outcome of all things regardless of which string we are in presently in our lives. Moving us from one string to another is His job and, as a result, He can make changes in our existence if we have faith in Him. I am sure many will disagree, and I am not trying to create a new alien theology, but I believe faith precedes knowledge, at least knowledge of God and perhaps of our own life as well. The Scripture says in 1 Corinthians 8:1, "Knowledge puffs up (pride), but love edifies."

We are his creation, not the creator. Pride makes us want to think that we can become the creator of all we see with our eyes and, somehow, through our growing knowledge eventually understand everything. This is very illogical to me.

Scripture says in Psalm 33:9 that God spoke, and it came to be. I know the Bible has much to say about this topic, but I believe we are spiritual beings having a physical experience. Our core nature is spiritual not physical. Life here on earth is but a passing breath of air. My seventy-five years compared to eternity is nothing. James 4:14 says, "What is your life? It is a vapor that appears for a little time and then vanishes away." I am here today and gone tomorrow. Think logically. I do. If God created us, and He is a loving God, wouldn't he also provide us with a way to know Him? Yes, I think so, and it has been here since the beginning and is here now in Scripture. We must pray to Him as He has instructed, and ask, seek, and believe what He has told us in order to find Him and know Him.

There is really nothing religious about this. It is not a form of godliness, where we go through traditionally human rituals to somehow attain knowledge of our creator through all the material things we create.

God's Work of Art

I often wake up in the night with new understanding and revelations from the Lord.

Recently, I was troubled by a comment from a dear brother, who I respect greatly, who said, "No one wants to see your dirty laundry, Ray." Regardless, I could not find that in Scripture. I forgave my brother and went to sleep, but had become discouraged and even started questioning whether I was to write this book.

I awoke at about 4:00 AM as I often do when God wants to encourage me. He told me to get the camera on my iPhone and take a picture of the lower left corner of a painting print I have hung in my sitting room.

The painting by Camille Pissarro is called *The Garden of Les Mathurins at Pontoise*. I like Pissarro's work since it is often very colorful. Here is the full painting.

As I pondered what I was doing and looking at, the Lord spoke to me and said that my life was like a beautiful painting. After coming to the Cross and repenting of what was left of the un-mentionables and D in my life, He allowed me to see the painting of my life from His perspective. After all, He is the artist, we are the canvas.

Then, He explained that if I only focused on the small dark portion of the painting in the lower left corner, and tried to myself change the colors from dark to light, I would merely become discouraged. Of course, I would fail since I am not the artist.

Furthermore, if I only focused on the bright colorful portion of the painting and myself tried to add more colors, I would become proud of my work and fail as well. Once again, I am not the artist.

Then, He said, both portions of the painting are His workmanship. They are the same work of art. It was at that point I realized the entire story of my life had to be told which included the good, the bad, and the ugly. It also had to be told from His viewpoint, not mine.

Ephesians 2:10 says, "For we are God's workmanship, created in Christ Jesus for good works, which God prepared beforehand that we should walk in them." Discouragement left and I had new resolve to finish writing.

Distractions in My Life

When I was set free from my sin, I began to realize how many things had distracted me from the pure and wonderful experience of knowing my creator through Jesus, also my Savior and Lord.

- TV shows
- Extraterrestrial ideologies
- Daily negative and fearful news
- Political infighting
- Scam calls on my landline and cellphone
- My iPhone and all the apps, reminders, and ads
- The urgencies of the moment, like repairs which are nonessential
- Do this, do that
- Meetings

- Cleaning
- Organizing
- Hobbies
- Tasks needed to be done
- On and on

These are all what God was showing me were idols in my life. None produced fruit or godly behavior but only more obsession and stress. When I let them order and rule my life, they only produced death in me.

Ninety percent or more of the news today produces fear, not faith. The Oscars and Emmys promote pride and arrogance, devil worship, not humility. Constant commercials produce idolatry. Drag race shows openly promote homosexual behavior and perversion. And, almost everything on television is peppered with partial and lewd behavior or nudity, including the half-time show at the Super Bowl or shows like *Naked and Afraid*. I thought watching or listening to these things would be harmless and somehow make my life more fulfilled.

When I watched these, the images became a part of me, not God. The Bible again is correct when it says in 1 Peter 5:8, Be alert and of sober mind. Your enemy, the devil, prowls around like a roaring lion looking for someone to devour. I want to become a friend of God, not a friend of the devil.

All these things were always trying to shove their way ahead of the real task of worshipping God through music, praying, reading His Word in the Scripture, listening for Him to speak to me and waiting to sense His presence and receive answers, and knowing when I had heard His voice.

Some, like tasks, have their rightful place; but, they were never to be first but second. The Scripture says, in Proverbs 3:5–6, to trust in the Lord with all your heart, lean not on your own understanding, but in all your ways acknowledge Him, and He will direct your paths. To me, this means if I place Him first in everything, His path for my life will be ordered as He sees and I will experience His presence and blessing in all I do. I can't acknowledge God while I vape or while I watch porn or do any of the other things I did. It does not work.

Who is the source of all these disruptions, especially in today's world? It is definitely not God, so it must be the enemy of God or Satan and his satanic hoard of demons.

My Prayer of Praise

I love to listen to a music sung by Marty Goetz. His compilation of songs called *I Call You Friend* always encourages me, builds me up, and makes me cry with thanksgiving. I recommend it for anyone like me. In the morning, when I worship, I listen to his music, and it so exactly depicts who the Lord is and what He has done in my life, I always weep tears of joy.

I start all my times with the Lord with worship, both in the morning and in the evening before bed. Sometimes I sing, off key, my own psalms, whatever comes to my mind, and I always feel God's presence soon after. I once experienced accompanying angels singing along, and found my worshipping was surprisingly in key. Sometimes, I sing in tongues, if I do not have any words. It has the same effect.

Worship is precious to God, and it is awesome to me because, through it, I enter His presence. My new normal is worship followed by prayer followed by the study of Scripture.

Psalm 22:3 states that God inhabits the praises of His people.

My Editor and Forever Friend Bob (Ace) Merritt

I have known Bob since I was about eleven or twelve years old when my parents moved down the street from him and his mom. He is a powerhouse for God. As youths, we both became amateur radio operators along with another close friend named

Bob, played musical instruments together, him on the trumpet and myself on the clarinet, hiked together to twin bridges, and often discussed life. We both owned telescopes and enjoyed stargazing and looking at the craters on the moon. We attended the same high school and church. Upon graduating, he attended West Point and became a champion marksman, hence, his name became "Ace."

When young, I remember hikes together to Twin Bridges in Des Moines where we would watch the slowly moving freight trains go by and, sometimes, even jump on one and off again. We also would lay pennies on the tracks and pick them up later flattened like a pancake. Other childlike antics included lighting small firecrackers and stuffing them in each other's back pockets and laughing at the results. We also would pass gas and see who could create the largest flame thrower from behind us. No Internet or iPhones in those days, but we made our own excitement.

After I realized I was a descendant of William Brewster, I remembered Ace telling me that he was a descendant of Brewster. That brought me comfort knowing we had a relational link even though it was centuries in the past.

We lost contact until early 2001, when I called West Point to try to locate him. I located Bob and we were reunited in Florida. My son David accompanied me on the trip. Later, on two occasions, Bob came to visit me in my new house in New Hampshire. Jane also met him at that time.

On the first visit, I invited a third friend, Dick Brown, whom we had known in Des Moines. At the time Bob visited, Dick lived near me in New Hampshire. Dick played the drums, Ace tooted on the trumpet, and I played the clarinet. The three of us would practice together.

When we met and sat together discussing old times, and they joked about my obsessive orderliness, Bob and Dick began discussing the Bible. Dick was a former Air Force pilot and later airline pilot who flew the same plane and route, before retiring, from Boston to Heathrow in Britain. This was one of the flights which crashed into the World Trade Center. Anyway, Dick had studied and become fluent in Hebrew and conducted Bible studies in his home in New Hampshire. I listened as Ace and Dick debated Scripture, remaining pretty quiet but in awe at God's work.

On the second visit, I remember Ace being as bold as a lion, witnessing to an attendant deep cleaning my car at the car wash. He later boldly witnessed to our mutual friends at our fiftieth reunion gathering. He later labeled me the "reunionater." That made me chuckle. I always respected Ace, because he graduated in the top 5% of our high school class of over 600. He was one smart cookie. He also became involved in our weekly Zoom meeting with Bob Mendelsohn, from Jews for Jesus, as we study various Old Testament books in the Bible. Ace always asks deep questions, revealing his Bible knowledge.

What I did not know until recently was that he was an editor for Hewlett-Packard and also edited a book written by another classmate, Steve Druker, entitled **Altered Genes, Twisted Truth,** which was endorsed by Jane Goodall. She is recognized as one of the foremost experts on chimpanzees.

I was honored when Ace agreed to edit my book and write a section on how to start your journey with God. He is my friend forever.

The Fear of God to Me

One Bible verse that recently helped me finally abandon the THC vaping, cloaked as medical, and porn, on a zip drive, is Matthew 7:22, which, in short, says, Many will say to Me in that day, Lord, Lord, have we not prophesied in Your name, cast out demons in Your name, and done many wonders in Your name, and then I will declare to them, I never knew you, depart from

Me, you who practice lawlessness. This scared the "bajeebies" out of me.

Regardless of the theological discussions of whether I ever did know God at all, and whether He knew me, I started praying fervently, that I come to know God so that I could hear His voice again, instead of running and hiding, and that I would begin to trust Him in every area and truly believe His words and obey His voice in my heart.

Of course, He knows all of us, He created us, but I am not into gambling today when it comes to eternal life versus destruction. Perhaps this is the fear of God which was the beginning of a little wisdom in me. His ways are not ours. I boasted about things, in pride, covering up my own hurting and problems rather than confessing my hidden sins and unmentionables and believing that knowing Him and Him knowing me would *far* surpass the feelings of euphoria I experienced by committing the unmentionables.

I am now back to where I was when I first believed. I am hearing His clear voice in my spirit and fellowshipping with Him daily. I am actually much closer to God than when I first believed. He has always been working in me. I don't experience guilt from my former sins anymore. I cannot tell you how awesome this is. The more deeply honest I become with Him, my own self, and others, the more He reveals Himself to me, including His works of mercy, love, and transformation in my life. Now, at age seventy-five, I am done with any unmentionables. I no longer experience the endless cycle of sin, suffer guilt, repent, and then repeat. I don't fear death as I did at age four.

Do I still have other areas today where I need sanctification? Of course, but I am much quicker to turn them over to God, repent or change my mind, and obey His voice realizing I will know Him even better. Just like the annual sacrifices offered in the Temple to cleanse the Israelites of their sins, He is our eternal sacrifice if we believe in Him and walk with Him.

Scripture says that the fear of the Lord is the beginning of wisdom. I thought I feared God, but the kind of fear I had was only the fear of being eternally disciplined to a burning hell. I believed that due to my behavior I deserved to suffer in hell. However, it never produced in me any lasting righteousness or sanctification in the area of the unmentionables. So, what is the fear of God to me today? It is knowing that God has worked throughout my life showing me His deep mercy, grace, and awesome love, and is continually showing these things to me today. His grace, mercy, and love will continue into my future. For me, the fear of God is being separated from Him forever in the future. After seeing what I have seen, these things bring me great fear.

This, for me, is the fear of the Lord; and, it has produced the beginning of wisdom. The Scripture in Psalm 130: 3–4 states, "If You, Lord, should mark iniquities, O Lord, who could stand? But there is forgiveness with You, That You may be feared."

CHAPTER 5

Finally, New Beginnings at Age Seventy-Five

When I came to the Cross, and God prompted me to make a decision between Him and following my lusts, I finally made the correct decision. This was more serious than I had ever heard Him nudge me before, and it was more difficult for me than I had ever experienced. I destroyed over $1,000 of THC cartridges and $212 of Caverject Impulse and crushed the USB stick with all the porn. At that point, instantly, my life took a radical turn. I was restored, and I remembered how it was when I was saved during my lunch break at Funeral Security Plans; but, this time, I knew I was healed, delivered, and sanctified. Here were the results.

- I have been given the gift of celibacy with peace of mind.
- Lust of the flesh, especially of the eyes, was removed and replaced with an ability to look into others' eyes and appreciate their inner qualities.

- Kindness replaced anger towards everyone, even wild drivers on the highway to Boston.
- Mercy and kindness replaced my judgment and criticism of others, especially those who I felt hurt me in my past.
- God revealed how He had answered all my prayers over the years in His way, not mine.
- My soul and my memory were restored, enabling me to remember people and their names and places and events all the way back to my childhood.
- Faith in God to lead me in my endeavors, daily, hourly, and every minute replaced anxiety and obsessive-compulsive behavior.
- I had received His gift of pcacc that surpasses all understanding.
- The Scriptures in the Bible came alive as He led me to new verses I had never seen before.
- I was given joy unspeakable and full of glory, crying daily ever since with gratitude and joy for what He had done.
- I was given an honest heart and faith to boldly write about what I had done wrong and all He had done in me since I was born.
- I was able to hear His clear still small voice and see His miraculous working in each daily life event in my life.
- I gained new Christian friends and some old friends were restored.
- The desire and habitual use of D was replaced with minimal pain and removal of any desire to return to using.
- Anger and guilt were replaced with compassion and mercy toward others.
- Judgment of myself for my past ceased and was replaced with acceptance and faith in the future.
- I was given faith that replaced all kinds of fears—especially of dying, failing to succeed, getting COVID, and being

nuked—as well as fearing what others thought of me when I exposed myself to them.

- Joy has replaced depression.
- Honesty replaced lying.
- Confidence was given to me that my name is written in God's Book of Life.
- I was given a vision of the rest of my life and assured that I would die in my sleep at home, not in a nursing home or on my way to a hospital or in the hospital.
- I no longer was interested in any of the unmentionables.
- I was given the gift of kindness and love for others without judgment toward them for anything, behavior, appearance, or nationality.
- I realized how God had already begun to fulfill in me what is spoken of in 2 Peter 1:5–8, the progression to knowing Him and becoming fruitful.
- He gave me faith to just show kindness and love toward others versus preaching at them.
- Anger toward adverse circumstances has nearly disappeared.
- Rest and trust have replaced my obsessive-compulsive behavior.
- My new routine in the morning involves worship, prayer while listening for God to speak to me, reading Scripture and then a good book, before doing other things.
- In the evening, before going to bed, I worship and pray.
- I enjoy giving more than getting.
- I have returned to my first love and distractions no longer distract me from God and His priorities.
- God is first in my life.
- Joy has replaced depression.
- I daily see more things that He has done and is doing in me.

- God has become my friend through Jesus, Yeshua, my Messiah.

Perhaps the greatest and most wonderful thing which has occurred to me is knowing I am able to hear His voice and walk with Him throughout the day.

I am no exception. I still have areas which I daily take to the Lord, and He quickly forgives me and gives me confidence and faith to continue my journey without repeating the same mistakes again. I tell people and my family that I feel better than I have for sixty years.

My friend Bob Mendelsohn, of Jews for Jesus Australia and Asia, recently recommended a book called **Gentle and Lowly**, written by Dane Ortlund. I recommend it to anyone who has struggled in areas as I have.

My boasts and failures have become God's testimony through me, His vessel of mercy. My life is a small subset of His wonderful autobiography.

The meaning of my English name, Ray, is "a beam of light." I certainly never thought of myself as light for anyone, especially a beam of light, like a lighthouse providing guidance for ships at sea. I perceived myself only as darkness. It is wonderful that God does not look at us as we do.

In Genesis 4:17, Abraham was given a new name and, in Genesis 17:15, Sarah was given a new name as well. I believe God inspires our parents to give us meaningful names. I am no exception. Furthermore, in Romans 4:17, God declares things that are not as though they are. I accept God's given name and its meaning for me in my life today. He has declared things that were not as though they were, and they became real visible light in me. I am no exception.

My life, as well as everyone's life, is like a beautiful painting. If we take a magnifying glass and only look at a one-inch by one-inch square of the painting, we may see dark brush marks or beautiful colored brush marks. However, to appreciate the artist's work, one needs to view the entire painting.

Until God opened my eyes, I only viewed the dark brush marks, not the total picture He was painting, and, for a few more years, He is still painting me.

The darkness in me has been exposed and has turned into His glorious light or understanding.

I love my life today, and I see every dark tunnel as an opportunity for God to reveal His light in and through me to others as I continue my walk with Him daily.

How Do I Begin My Journey or Restore My Journey with God

In the anecdote, **"Hope in the Midst of More Failure"** in chapter 2, I mentioned that I did not find God by attending church. Later, my wife Debbie and I did find a good church which we attended for ten years. This was after my second birth experience.

Finding a good local church that teaches from Scripture is important to promote continual Christian growth after you begin your journey with God.

As my sister had told me, I suggest you purchase an easy to read Bible. I read the Living Bible, although many would say this is not an accurate version, it certainly led me to God and it can be read like an ordinary book. Today, I read the New King James version which is a more accurate translation than the Living Bible.

If you are desperate like I was, pray to God in Yeshua's name or Jesus' name and ask Him to open the eyes of your heart to know Him as you read. This is essential! Resist doubts that enter into your mind stating that God will not or could not answer your prayer due to the horrific sins you may have committed. God is full of awesome mercy and has great love for all of us as it states in Ephesians 2:4.

Reading the Bible is key to understanding who God is. It is also the key to restoring a relationship with Him. The words, although written by men, are totally inspired by God. It is not a natural book but a supernatural book. Resist all temptations to doubt its content and effectiveness to change your life.

If you're desperate like I was, it will not matter what people think or say about it or about you reading the Bible. Deny your doubts and unbelief by reading it! Let the Scripture create faith in you as you read it! Expect a miracle to occur! It will! Realize that God is alive and well and wants to reveal Himself to all of us when we ask, seek, and find as stated in Matthew 7:7. He is able and willing to speak to us through His words in Scripture.

You may want to begin reading the book of John or Matthew in the New Testament. If you are Jewish, begin by reading Isaiah 53 or Zechariah 12:10. Then, read the New Testament. Read John 3, especially John 3:16, to understand the second birth experience.

As you read, pray and ask God questions. Then, expect Him to answer your questions through Scripture or directly in His still small voice. He will, and His answers will agree with Scripture.

Think logically. I have a very logical mind, and I wanted answers that made sense. I deduced that either, Scripture is a pack of lies or it is ALL truth. There is no in-between. Jesus says in John 14:6, "I am the way, the truth, and the life. No one comes to the father except through me." If one Scripture is not true, then the whole Bible is false. Proverbs 30:5 says, "Every word of God is pure." Hebrews 4:12 says, "For the word of God is living and powerful, and sharper than any two-edged sword, piercing even to the division of soul and spirit, and of joints and marrow, and is a discerner of the thoughts and intents of the heart."

As you struggle with your specific issues in life, whether sins like mine or depression, fear, anxiety, sickness, or complacency, expect God's love to overcome these things. It will! Romans 8:38–39 states, "For I am persuaded that neither death nor life, nor angels nor principalities nor powers, nor things present, nor things to come, nor height nor depth, nor any other created thing, shall be able to separate us from the love of God which is in Christ (Messiah) Jesus (Yeshua) our Lord." My story is proof in the pudding.

Believe that knowing Jesus is far greater and more exciting and fulfilling than any D or unmentionables or any worldly pleasure. I have experienced this and I am no exception. Continue doing the above until you experience God in your life.

As you begin each day, look for new and exciting things to occur! Maybe, an old friend will call or, maybe, you will have a new peace in your heart or, possibly, you will have faith you've never experienced. Maybe God will reveal Himself through an event or circumstance. Perhaps, you will begin to see things differently than you have in the past. It will occur! Do not give up or quit until it does! He wants to change your heart so that the things which you once loved which don't align with His Word are gone.

Do not let religion drive you away from God. Religion to me is trying to reach God on my terms by my good behavior or works. This is based in pride and is not the way God brings change in our lives. Scripture teaches in Romans 2:4 that "knowing that the goodness of God Leads you to repentance."

Finally, be thankful to God. You can say it simply, "Jesus loves me. This I know, for the Bible tells me so." Give Him thanks versus profanity and watch profanity disappear.

Continue doing the aforementioned progressively, more and more, throughout your life and you will become a friend of the Lord and experience His love in your hearts and the freedom from whatever problems you have.

If you want to know God in a personal, intimate way, here is prayer to begin your life with Him.

Jesus, Yeshua, I have sinned in many ways and fallen short of your requirements in Scripture.

I confess my sins to you and change my mind and turn from my sins knowing that you are a merciful, loving God, full of grace, desiring to bless me with a new life and fellowship with you.

Forgive me for my sins and cleanse me with your blood shed on the Cross and come into my heart and take charge of my life.

In Jesus', Yeshua's name.

Tell someone you have accepted Christ and are now a Christian.

Have faith, or believe, you are now saved.

Begin reading Scripture as mentioned and find a good church.

Acknowledgments

MY SISTER SUZANNE BLAZER, who never gave up praying and sharing her hope in Christ to me and my family. Our reuniting will be soon.

My father, who gave his life to Jesus just before passing and saw an angel waiting at the foot of his bed. Dad, I am coming home soon.

My mom, who tolerated my nonsense for years, but always gave so much, not asking anything in return. Mom, I hope to ask forgiveness from you in person soon.

Jane, my closest friend for the past twenty-one years, who may not have agreed with my theology, but exhibits Christian love through her generosity: monetarily, many years ago, enabling me to buy the house I live in today and, especially, her total lack of interest in hearing about my past. Thank you for riding with me, and being there through this crazy, oftentimes scary, life. I love you, Jane, with Christ's love.

My pastor, Sean Theodore, of Abundant Grace Fellowship, who preaches the pure word of Scripture without compromise.

My dear Messianic Jewish friend, Bob Mendelsohn, who I knew years ago, but have been reunited with on a weekly Zoom meeting for the past two years. His heart of compassion and love toward others and myself has revealed God's great mercy and forgiveness to me. And, he has a wonderful sense of humor. He inspired me to write about my life.

Ace (Bob) Merritt, my close friend, neighbor as a youth, fellow ham, fellow musician, and often an inspiration to me, and, sixty-five years later, a prayer partner and companion on the weekly Jews for Jesus Zoom study meetings. Bob is a West Point graduate and a marksman with a pistol, hence, the name "Ace." He is bold as a lion, with a lamb's heart. Looking forward to our reuniting in the future.

Marty Goetz, whom I have not met, but whose music inspires me and draws me daily closer to God and Yeshua, our Messiah.

Lou Poggi, my Christian friend, who has faithfully maintained my pool since 2004 and brings with him nuggets of wisdom appropriate for me throughout the year.

Anne Parker Pohl, my first cousin, closest to me today, who has had her physical battles but is more than a conqueror through Christ.

Tom Hunter, my cousin, who lent me money to enable me to start over in a new job in Colorado Springs.

Ann Hunter Fuller, my cousin, who opened her home to my son David and me several years ago when I was being restored.

Horacio Attore, my Italian barber, who always greets me with a smile; asks how are you doing, how are the kids and Jane; and, shares openly his life experiences.

Karen Mitchell, a Christian prayer warrior, who helped me understand Romans 8:1, which always brought me condemnation.

Jacob Stanley Thompson, my grandson, who, like a beacon, shines with the love of Christ for his papa (grandfather).

My former wife Deborah, also a prayer warrior, who has forgiven me and has a deep heart of compassion for everyone, the Jew first and also the Greek or Gentile.

My children, who have suffered much because of my past but never hesitated to call me out when I was wrong and have often been there when I needed them. I deeply love each of you, especially today.

My nephew Denny Thompson, whose story of a Des Moines marathon he ran inspired me to keep running the race of life and whose humor, when a missionary with His wife in Uganda, surpassed many I have known.

Sol, my house cleaning helper.

Denny's wife, Sandra Thompson, whose love for people, prayers, and encouragement through Facebook kept me going.

My nephew Chris Blazer, who took time from his schedule to visit me in New Hampshire from Kansas City.

My Christian friends over the years, but especially those with whom I have been reunited on Facebook.

Arthur Katz, who I had the pleasure of knowing years ago for a short time and who openly shared his struggles with me, providing encouragement. Art, I am excited about our reuniting.

Dr. Andrew Meyers, who showed compassion and gave a listening ear during many difficult times. Andy, a few more years, and I will thank you in person.

Gordon Lewis, who shared an edible flower with me and his love for bees and flowers and the only person I have met in seventy-five years with the same nickname as myself, "Buppy."

Pastor Ernie Gruen, my first pastor, of Full Faith Church of Love, who left a legacy for me to follow even with his own difficult struggles. Pastor Ernie, I'll see you again soon.

Elder William Brewster, Chief Elder and *Mayflower* passenger, my tenth great-grandfather, whose life experiences and even death experience as recorded have been such a great inspiration to my walk. Great-grandfather William, I cannot wait to meet you.

Mary and Kate Parker, my wonderful friends since preschool and fishing buddies as kids and fierce competitors when playing

Monopoly, Clue, and Chutes and Ladders at their Clear Lake home. We will meet again later.

Bill Bryson, who I have never met, but whose anecdotes as a child also growing up in Des Moines, as written in his book **The Thunderbolt Kid**, so paralleled mine that I gave copies to each of my children so they knew what my grade school years were like.

Jim Ryun, whose life has inspired me to finish the race and complete the course.

Dane Ortlund, whose book *Gentle and Lowly* helped me understand the extent of God's mercy and grace.

Yeshua, Jesus, my Savior and Lord, who loves me, saved me from destruction, wrote my name in His Book of Life, and who lives with me and in me now here in Derry. You are the first I want to meet in the future.

So many others whose names or encounters I have forgotten, but will remain in my heart.

www.ingramcontent.com/pod-product-compliance
Lightning Source LLC
Chambersburg PA
CBHW051718090426
42738CB00010B/1968